NEW YORK CRIME

FROM TRUANCY TO CRIME

B
81
53
28

THE CRIME COMMISSION OF NEW YORK STATE

FROM TRUANCY TO CRIME — A STUDY OF 251 ADOLESCENTS

BY THE SUB-COMMISSION ON CAUSES AND EFFECTS OF CRIME

1928

ALBANY
J. B. LYON COMPANY, PRINTERS
1928

LB
3081
.N53
1928

CRIME COMMISSION

CALEB H. BAUMES, Chairman
BURTON D. ESMOND, Vice-chairman

B. ROGER WALES,   WM. LEWIS BUTCHER,
WALTER S. GEDNEY,   JANE M. HOEY,
DAVID S. TAYLOR,   JOHN KNIGHT,
THOMAS S. RICE,   JOSEPH A. McGINNIES.
GEORGE F. CHANDLER

HERBERT L. SMITH, Secretary
Senate Chamber, Albany

SUB-COMMISSION

WM. LEWIS BUTCHER, Chairman
JANE M. HOEY,   JOSEPH A. McGINNIES.

ASSISTANTS
RAYMOND MOLEY,   HARRY M. SHULMAN,
Research Advisor.   Research Worker.

A REPORT OF THE SUB-COMMISSION ON CAUSES AND EFFECTS OF CRIME

LETTER OF TRANSMITTAL

To the Crime Commission of New York State:

From truancy to crime—a study of 251 adolescents, answers for at least the group of cases studied, two questions of paramount interest to all who are interested in crime prevention. First—what happens in afteryears to children who are dealt with as juvenile delinquents; second—what facts in their histories or background were significant in differentiating those who grew up to be criminals, from the others.

This study, based on cases taken from the files of the Bureau of Attendance of the New York City Schools, was made and the report written by Harry M. Shulman, research worker for the Sub-Commission on Causes, under the direction of the members of the Sub-Commission. Professor Raymond Moley acted in an advisory capacity.

Dated, February 28, 1928.

WM. LEWIS BUTCHER, *Chairman*,
JANE M. HOEY,
JOSEPH A. McGINNIES,
Sub-Commission.

LB
3081
.N53
1928

FROM TRUANCY TO CRIME—A STUDY OF 251 ADOLESCENTS

INTRODUCTION

The newspapers print daily stories dealing with "crime waves" and with "juvenile crime waves" which give the impression that there are tremendous fluctuations in the degree of lawlessness of our citizens. As a matter of fact, this is not true. Estimates made by criminologists of the portion of the population habitually engaged in crime vary only slightly, some placing the figure at one per cent, and others at between one and two per cent.[1]

Crime statistics, however, indicate that this group, most of whom are repeated offenders, begin their careers at comparatively early ages, and commit new offenses of increased severity and with greater frequency, with advancing years. It is this development of criminal careers that constitutes a real crime wave, one which begins in childhood, increases during adolescence, continues mounting during the years of vigorous manhood, and ebbs only as old age approaches.

Whether this curve, which follows the life curve, rising as life expands and gains power over its surroundings, and declining as life ebbs in the human body, takes its shape because of hereditary and physical factors or because of influences of social origin, in the home, in school, in industry, or in idle and spare time is still an open question.

Of practical importance is the question of how this curve may be modified. Common sense dictates that the solution lies in preventing or curing criminal tendencies among the young. But here the problem still remains of discovering which influences are aids and which are hindrances to sound and healthy growth.

The present study is an attempt within limited time and space to give consideration to the subsequent careers of a group of children known to be juvenile delinquents six years ago. This study concerns itself with the growth of the crime curve among this group, the apparent influence upon the curve of certain objectively measurable environmental factors, and the relation among this group of early childhood habits of delinquency to the growth of the curve in adolescence. Because of the difficulties involved, the study has been limited sharply in character and concerns itself only with the histories of two hundred and fifty-one truant boys, in the Borough of Manhattan, all of whom had experienced commitments to the Truant School because of chronic illegal absence from school. The survey covers their histories from the time of release from Truant School to the present date, a period of six to eight years, and reviews their more remote childhood.

(1) Parsons, Philip A.—Crime and the Criminal 1926, pp. 143, 147.

The obstacles to this study have been legion. Mobility in population, inaccuracy of records, conflicts in testimony taken from records, difficulties due to various spellings of proper names, all have hindered progress. Devising means of tracing families that had moved from old neighborhoods, sifting data for errors and checking against the inclusion of data on families with identical names, have taken a great deal of time and attention.

The burden of analyzing thousands of pages of information, summarizing them and tabulating the results has been lightened through the splendid assistance given by official and unofficial agencies and by volunteers, including students in social science courses. More than a hundred individuals have contributed their share to this study. Without them it would not have been completed.

THE FINDINGS

The report herewith presented gives conclusive evidence that among the cases studied, chronic truancy was in a disquieting number of cases, the first step in a criminal career. Fifty-one per cent of the boys required the attention of police and courts during the six to eight year period subsequent to their release from the Truant School, in the following division: juvenile delinquency, 21 per cent; adult offenders, 30 per cent. Among the adult offenders, 16 per cent committed offenses of minor character and 14 per cent were arraigned for felony offenses of the type usually committed by professional criminals.

Based on estimates of criminologists that 1 per cent of the population of the United States engage in some form of crime, the group of 251 truants were responsible during this limited period of from six to eight years, for 14 times as many felons as arise from the population at large.

Statistical study of 34 environmental and behavior factors in these cases indicates that only a limited number of these factors served to differentiate the truants who became adult offenders from those who, as a group, did not. Felonies were committed more, in proportion, by sons of natives and of remote immigrants —that is, by persons acquainted with the ways of the land, whereas minor infractions were committed in greater proportion by sons of recently arrived immigrants.

The proportion of families, one or more of whose members had police records, ranged from .43 for those boys who had no records subsequent to truancy, to .83 for those who became felons. Thus the boys who became serious offenders had the worst criminal family backgrounds.

On the other hand, the survey showed that almost the entire group of cases lived under conditions of extreme poverty and unusually congested housing, in homes that were broken by death or desertion of one or both parents in over one-half of the cases, and in which parental care was rendered ineffective in a large percentage of the cases by the employment of mothers at jobs in addition to household tasks.

The study shows therefore that most of the factors were influential only as general factors. It is true that the sordid conditions depicted were the soil from which an unusual amount of criminal behavior has sprung. It is likewise true that the conditions are similar to those to which the under-privileged group in any community are subjected, and that poverty and crime are associated in a general way. But in the group forming this study, as well as among the under-privileged group in general, the majority of the factors here studied throw no light on the reasons why certain families fostered criminal behavior and others did not, nor why one child reared in the same family under the self-same general conditions became a criminal and his brothers did not.

THE CONCLUSIONS

Three chief methods are being used in combating crime. They are the processes of legal procedure, of social reform, and of individual study and treatment. The method of legal procedure, while necessary, is as shown in this study, apparently not effective in preventing further crime among young offenders. The method of social reform is concerned with broad measures of social welfare, aimed at general factors influencing crime and not at specific experiences influencing criminals. The method of individual study and treatment gives the greatest promise of success in preventing crime. This method, represented in the procedure of physicians, psychiatrists, psychologists and social workers, has in recent years gained great strength in the United States, as attested to by the increasing number of philanthropic organizations, privately and publicly and endowed clinics, and federal, state and municipal bureaus concerned with the study and guidance of juvenile delinquents and adult criminals.

The individual method is concerned with the measure of individual limitations in capacity for social adjustment, with the discovery of the motives leading to anti-social behavior, and with methods of treatment that will utilize in a social way the normal drives of unadjusted persons. This method has practical limitations because of the expense involved and the lack of persons trained in its technique. However, the expense and time consumed have been justified by the aid which the individual findings have given to the understanding and control of larger groups. To mention only two outstanding examples, the psychological classification by ability of soldiers in the United States draft army of 1917 and 1918 and the classification of students under the modern educational methods used in many schools, have been products of years of arduous laboratory and clinic work in individual study and measurement.

The expense of the individual method is probably less than the costs of crime to society, per criminal. The annual cost of crime in the United States is estimated at billions of dollars. The individual method is probably less expensive than the method of legal procedure. In the 251 cases studied, no less than 679 arraignments before educational and judicial authorities took place, and 460 commitments were made to various reformatory and penal institutions. The process of arraigning and maintaining these boys must have cost incalculable thousands. The community has been re-imbursed through fines to the extent of $368.

Surely New York City, with its willingness to tear down old structures to make place for new, must concede the like importance of tearing down old methods when they stand in the way of progress. There is no doubt that present methods of dealing with crime among the youth of that city are wasteful of money and of careers. There is no doubt that the time to institute modern methods of child guidance is during childhood. There is no doubt that the school system is the place to begin the method. A decent consideration for our wayward children, if not for our own security and peace of mind, requires that we inaugurate such methods without further delay.

SUMMARY OF FINDINGS
I—A Statistical Analysis of Offenses

1. *Present Age of Offenders*

The non-delinquents, misdemeanants and felons were, on the average, of the same age. The juvenile delinquents were a year younger. These had not been arraigned for any offenses for four years. The conclusion is that the groups are sufficiently similar in age to make the differences in conduct between them, true differences, and the groups themselves distinct in their responses to social situations.

2. *Parentage*

Fifteen per cent of the group were of native parentage and eighty-five per cent were of foreign parentage. The nationality distribution of foreign-born parents in this group is an accurate sampling of nationality statistics for 4,476 children committed as truants during 1918–1922 inclusive, throughout New York City.

3. *Total number of Arraignments*

This group of 251 cases have been arraigned a total of 679 times, divided as follows:

Truancy 377
Juvenile Delinquency...................... 130
Misdemeanors 117
Felonies 55

124 cases or .49 had no court records subsequent to truancy.
127 cases or .51 had court records subsequent to truancy, as follows:

54—or .21 were juvenile delinquents
38—or .16 were arraigned as misdemeanants
35—or .14 were arraigned as felons

Thus, .30 of the cases were adult offenders. Criminologists estimate that one per cent of the population of the United States are offenders. On this basis, the group of 251 truants contributed, in proportion, 30 times as many adult offenders as does the population at large.

4. *Proportion of Arraignments*

The felons were arraigned an average of five times, the misdemeanants an average of 4.3 times, the juvenile delinquents an average of three times and the truants an average of 1.4 during this 6 to 8 year period. Seriousness of offenses was accompanied by increased number of arraignments.

5. *Proportion of Arraignments by Type of Offense*

The delinquents appeared in the Children's Court three times as often as the misdemeanants and one and one-half times as often as the felons. The truant who is arraigned before the Children's Court is thus less apt to be an adult offender than the truant who is not.

The felons tended to commit felonies in greater number than misdemeanors, being arraigned twice as often for felonies as for misdemeanors.

6. *Nature of Delinquencies.*

The type of juvenile delinquencies committed by the juvenile delinquents, misdemeanants and felons would not have been any clue to their subsequent careers as more or less the same types of offenses were committed by all 3 groups.

7. *Misdemeanors*

Of 117 misdemeanors, 33 were committed by felons, and 84 by misdemeanants, despite the almost equal size of the two groups of young men.

8. *Nature of Felonies*

Eighty-one per cent of all felonies consisted of burglary, grand larceny and robbery, crimes involving violence or stealth.

9. *Convictions*

Convictions for previous offenses among the felons were as great as among the other groups. The felons became serious offenders in spite of contact with courts and institutions.

10. *Disposition of Cases*

The boys who became felons were in fewer number placed on probation, and were subjected to a greater number of institutional commitments than were the lesser offenders.

II—Social Factors

1. *Nativity of Parents and Offenders*

An average of .85 of the parents were foreign born and .82 of the offenders were native born.

The foreign born parents were approximately 25 per cent more numerous in the group studied than were foreign born adults in the total population of Manhattan Borough in 1920. Therefore, foreign parentage has significance as a factor influencing truant behavior.

There were six per cent more foreign born boys in the 251 cases studied than in the foreign born juvenile population of Manhattan in 1920.

The factor of foreign-born parentage was four times as frequent as that of foreign birth among the offenders.

The group of offenders committing misdemeanors have a greater proportion of foreign parents and a greater proportion of native children than the truancy and juvenile delinquency groups.

A comparison of nativity data on the 251 cases and on 4,476 cases committed to the Truant Schools during the period of 1918–1922 shows the present group to be an accurate sampling, for nativity.

2. *Recency of immigration among parents of offenders*

One-third of the parents arrived before 1900 and two-thirds after 1900, for the truancy, juvenile delinquent, and misdemeanor groups. Half arrived before 1900 and half after 1900 for the felony group. The felonies were committed more, in proportion, by sons of persons acquainted with the ways of the land, whereas minor infractions of the law were committed in greater proportion by sons of newly arrived immigrants.

3. *Number of Children in Family*

Parents whose sons were only truants and not more serious offenders had slightly smaller families than those whose sons were delinquent or criminal, the former average being 4.2 children and the latter 5.1 children.

4. *Position in Order of Birth in relation to Offenses*

The second child had the worst record for juvenile delinquencies, misdemeanors and felonies. The child least likely to be delinquent was the next youngest. The youngest child is less likely to be truant than the oldest and intermediate children.

Since most of the parents were of foreign birth and the earlier children were born when the families were least adjusted to the new country, the disproportionate amount of anti-social behavior of the earlier born might be attributed to the lack of social and economic adjustment of the recently arrived foreign born. The data on the felony group, however, does not fit this conclusion.

The youngest child tended to commit more offenses than the next youngest. This is contrary to the other data, and indicates that the psychology and sociology of the youngest child may be different than that of the other brothers and sisters.

5. *Income in Relation to Offenses*

Whether a boy will be a felon or only a truant did not seem to be affected by the size of the family income. In general, the whole group of 251 cases were from families of very low income. Poverty alone therefore is not a cause of crime, as non-offenders and offenders both came from the same economic group.

6. *Occupations of Mothers*

Forty-seven per cent of all mothers in this group of cases worked at jobs in addition to household tasks. Among the more serious offenders, the mothers did more home industry work than outside work. This seems contrary to common sense, but the explanation may be that the mothers working away from home made better provisions for the supervision of their children than those who merely added work to domestic duties.

7. *Status of Home*

In .52 of the families, the home status was impaired by the death or absence of one parent.

In .35 of the families, the home was broken, due to the death or absence of the father. In .17 of the families the mother was dead or absent.

The felony group, contrary to expectation, has a greater proportion of unbroken homes than other groups. This would indicate that the study of felony must go deeper than is possible in studies of this type. The number of homes where the mother was missing was disproportionately high in the truancy group, and homes where the father was missing were above average in the misdemeanor group.

8. *Degree of Housing Congestion*

There is no significant relation between the number of persons per room and severity of offenses. But in general, the group of 251 cases lived under conditions of housing congestion twice as great as the average poor in congested areas. Unspeakable congestion therefore must have had some relation to the truancy of this group, if not to severer offenses.

9. *Philanthropic Aid*

Seventy-five per cent or 188 of the families were known to social service agencies. Sixty-three were not known. An average of 2.8 registrations were made, on the families given attention, and a total of 435 registrations were made. Financial and medical aid were most frequently given. Specialized recreation and employment guidance registrations were very few in number. Families whose sons were juvenile and adult offenders received more aid than families whose sons were only truant.

10. *Mobility*

The families of juvenile delinquents tended to move less often than those of the other offense groups. This may account in part, for the disproportionate number of gangs among juvenile delinquency cases.

11. Extent of Criminal Record Among Families of Offenders

As severity of offenses among the cases increased, the number of families one or more of whose members had criminal records, increased. Thus, .43 of families of truants, .50 of families of juvenile delinquents, .66 of families of misdemeanants, and .83 of families of felons had criminal records.

III—Behavior Factors

12. Onset of Truancy

Truancy in all groups became a serious problem early in school life. Truants who became juvenile delinquents were serious truancy problems in grade 2-A, the misdemeanor and felony groups in 3-B, and the non-delinquent group in 3-A. The entire group became maladjusted to their school surroundings at an age so early that preventive work could undoubtedly have been carried out at that time with a great degree of success.

13. Degree of Truancy

The children who became serious offenders were on the average not more frequently truant than the others and no prognosis on this basis could have been possible.

14. Conduct marks given by teachers

The average conduct rating received by the group was "B". The misdemeanor group had somewhat less than its proper proportion of A's and the felons had slightly more than their proper proportion of C's. The differences were too small to be of much significance. These statistics show that the school ratings given by teachers were neither a real appraisal of the character nor a guide to the future conduct of the children.

15. Grade reached

There was no differentiation between offense groups on the basis of school grade reached.

16. Gang Affiliation

Fifty-four of the 251 cases are designated as having been gang members. The actual number who were gang members cannot be determined, as the other cases had no information as to whether gang affiliation existed or not.

Of the cases reported on, the juvenile delinquency group was highest, .40 being gang members.

17. Degree of Skill in Position Held

Over half of the cases reported upon engaged in unskilled work and a negligible number in skilled work, with the exception of the juvenile delinquency group, who tended to enter better occupations than any of the others, the truants included. The benefits of Children's Court treatment are presumably the explanation for the vocational adjustment of some of the juvenile delinquents. While the degree of intelligence of the members of the group is not known, and its capacity for training is therefore also unknown, there is evidence of economic waste and vocational maladjustment in the job careers of this group because of the frequency in change of position and the periods of unemployment.

RECOMMENDATIONS

Following its study of 201 Truants, the Sub-Commission on Causes summarized its findings and recommendations as follows:

"In the light of our study it would seem that the truant requires consideration from several angles. His intelligence, educational activities and aptitudes require the study of clinical psychologists. His emotional attitudes toward home, toward school, toward his playmates and toward his life plan, require the study of psychiatrists. A practical solution for his individual difficulties require, the co-operation of a staff of trained social workers. His physical condition * * * certainly needs the close scrutiny of physicians. Finally, the school administrator must be called into conference with other experts for an adaptation of the school program to meet the needs of these children.

"These various techniques resolve themselves into the component elements of mental hygiene clinics. Such clinics are needed and should be established in the school systems of this state. These clinics, in our opinion, should preferably be established in the schools rather than be organized as separate agencies, inasmuch as their purpose is to meet only the needs of school children. Again, by being established within public schools, these clinics will serve as educational centers for the teaching staff, as well as therapeutic centers for the pupils.

"The trend of thought in the Board of Education of New York City at the present time is toward providing probationary schools where problem children may be segregated, and be given various clinical examinations and treatment. The Sub-Commission on Causes, however, feels that more effective work can be done by providing clinical treatment under normal, every-day school conditions rather than under institutional conditions developing from a process of segregation of children presenting problems.

"The recommendations of the Sub-Commission on Causes, therefore are:

1. The establishment within the school system of clinics for the medical, psychological and psychiatric study of children presenting behavior problems.
2. A revision of the school curriculum to meet the needs of the large group of children who have not the capacity for ordinary academic training, due to defective mentality or emotional instability.
3. The two foregoing recommendations should be subjected to a careful analysis and evaluation by some competent agency either within or without the school system. Such a study should be undertaken soon after the initiation of the project itself.
4. The Bureau of Attendance, of the Board of Education of New York City should be provided with trained case workers

assigned limited case-loads, for the supervision of children who are persistently truant, or who present other behavior problems.

5. The funds necessary for the establishment of the facilities described in the four previous recommendations should come preferably from public sources, but should there be hindrances to the prompt availability of public funds, then it is strongly urged that generous private funds be made available for the initiation of these projects.''

The findings on the present study of 251 adolescents serve to convince the Sub-Commission on Causes of the accuracy of its earlier findings and lead it to repeat its earlier recommendations with still greater emphasis.

The greater depth and breadth of the present study lead to the following additional recommendations:

1. Because of the defective home life, extent of criminality among parents and brothers, the number of broken homes, and the great proportion of working mothers among these 251 cases, any program for their supervision must include a subsidiary program of education and rehabilitation for their families. It is recommended that the work of visiting teachers be extended to include the families, or the service of family welfare societies be enlarged to do more intensive work with delinquent families.

2. Philanthropic agencies should become more aware of the needs of problem children in the families under their care and amplify their own program, either directly or through co-operation with the schools, for the prompt and early treatment of behavior disorders.

3. Since truancy begins early in school life, the school clinic procedure should be undertaken with younger as well as with older children and since conduct marks have been useless as an index of future behavior, there should be substituted a more significant description of behavior, based upon the principles of mental hygiene and psychology. This will require giving psychological and mental hygiene training to teachers.

4. Since the group of cases as a whole was seriously maladjusted vocationally, both with regard to type and regularity of employment, a practical program of vocational analysis, training and placement should supplant the present course of instruction in the higher school grades, for boys whose academic careers show no aptitude for abstract studies or for skilled trades and professions.

MANNER OF SELECTION OF CASES

The study is limited to 251 consecutive cases of boys committed to the Truant schools of New York City and released in October 1922, or prior thereto. Thus, from the time of their release until the date of this investigation, at least five years had elapsed.

The cases are all of boys who were resident in New York County (Manhattan Borough), at the time of commitment for truancy. Their records were drawn in consecutive order from the files of the Bureau of Attendance of the New York City Board of Education. In order to complete the required number of cases, releases dating back to June, 1920, were drawn upon. The study represents, therefore, a cross section of truancy over a period of nearly two and a half years, in a single Borough of Greater New York. The limitation of cases to a single borough was partly for purposes of convenience, and helped materially in expediting the completion of the study through reduction of time needed for travel to homes and to agencies where case records were available.

It should be borne in mind, in addition, that in selecting cases from Manhattan Borough, an urban area was chosen that for multiplicity of social agencies rendering medical, financial, child guidance, foster-care, employment, recreational, and many other forms of aid, is probably unrivaled anywhere in the United States, and perhaps in the world. It is not possible to evaluate the work done by these agencies, individually, but it ought to be remembered that most of the families were known to social agencies, and that their careers were presumably subject to whatever influence these agencies could exert upon them.

METHODS USED IN THE STUDY

Both the cross-section and the historical methods have been used in analyzing the materials here presented. In a measure, the study utilizes the sociological approach, this method being represented by 16 items of information on which tabulations have been made. The remaining items represent a behavior approach, and consist of 18 tabulations of the behavior record on the group of cases. The sociological items are concerned with the influence upon the boys of the behavior of the other members of the family, particularly with regard to criminal acts, and of the social and economic status of the family.

The behavior items are concerned with the significance of boyhood behavior in relation to adolescent acts.

The study was planned in three divisions:

1. A statistical analysis of the delinquencies, misdemeanors, and felonies committed by the group.
2. A statistical study of the social factors, and of the behavior factors accompanying:
    a. Cases in which truancy had no subsequent record of juvenile delinquency or criminality.
    b. Cases in which truancy was succeeded by juvenile delinquency.
    c. Cases in which truancy was succeeded by misdemeanors, or by juvenile delinquency and misdemeanors.
    d. Cases in which truancy was succeeded by felonies or juvenile delinquencies and felonies or by juvenile delinquencies, misdemeanors and felonies.

3. A narrative report on fifty cases, consisting of every fifth case in the group.

SOURCES USED IN GATHERING DATA

For the first division of the study, that of criminal career, a thorough search was made into all possible sources of **authentic information**. The conduct rating of each boy was obtained from a verbatim copy of the child's school record, on file at the Bureau of Attendance. Here also were obtained items on the child's behavior at the time of truancy, his bad habits, and other traits showing personality maladjustment. From the Criminal Identification Bureau of the New York Police Department were obtained the list of juvenile delinquency, misdemeanor and felony charges against each individual.* Where finger-prints were available, as a result of conviction, the finger-print records of the New York City Police Department were searched for additional criminal offenses committed under true names or under aliases. The records of the Police Department were then compared with those at the Bureaus of Criminal Identification of the City Department of Correction, the Magistrate's Court and the State Department of Correction. In this manner, all convictions and all other charges not listed under assumed names committed in the State of New York were obtained.

For the second, or social division of the study, every possible source was checked for information. A detailed record was first compiled from the case files of the Bureau of Attendance. On a separate card for each boy were recorded the following items: First name, last name, father's first name, mother's first and maiden names, marital status of parents, present address, all previous addresses since the boy entered public school, the names and dates of birth of all brothers and sisters, the birth-date of the boy himself, the occupations of father and mother, race, religion, nativity, land of birth, of parents and boy, and special identifying details.

These data cards were in duplicate. One copy was sent to the Police Department, and was used in gathering from the police files the data for division one. The other copy was sent to the Social Service Exchange, the confidential registration bureau for all social service agencies doing work in Manhattan Borough. From this Exchange was obtained the list of all social service agencies who had ever registered as being interested in any of the families in the group. This process was helpful in adding to the data in division one. Thus, sixteen cases not recorded by the Police Department were found to have been registered by the Probation Department of the Children's Court, as having had juvenile delinquency arraignments.

---

* The police lists were subject to certain errors. In some instances, persons with similar names living in the same neighborhood were erroneously included, and in other instances, persons with other first names were added. These were eliminated.

Every social service agency was sent a form letter and a summary blank, and was requested to give a summary of the cases known to it. On certain agencies who had done work with many of the families, this request placed a burden greater than could be met by their available staffs. In these instances, the cases were summarized by graduate students in sociology whose services were secured by cooperation with the Department of Education of New York University. These students summarized over a hundred cases.

Vital information on the school history of the child, and on certain items in the family background were obtained from the Bureau of Attendance. A schedule containing more than twenty items was prepared on each child by the clerks of that Bureau.

Data on the third division, the cases reported in narrative form were obtained through home visits by staff workers for the Sub-Commission on Causes. In every case an attempt was made to learn the present status of the boy. Not always could the boy himself be interviewed, although many return visits were made. The problem of tracing the families on the basis of old addresses was most difficult. The first attempt, made through obtaining the latest addresses known to the School Census Board of the Board of Education, failed because the majority of the homes had not been registered in recent years. The second plan, that of writing to the school attended in 1921 by the youngest child in the family, was more successful. In a number of cases, however, the children had transferred to other schools, and subsequent inquiries brought few returns. Certain addresses were obtained from the records of social service agencies. Still others were taken from current Police Department records of arraignments. Despite the use of all these methods, only half of the group of 251 cases were traced to present addresses.

When all the data were compiled, they were arranged in case folders and analyzed by means of a schedule. This schedule contained thirty-four items selected as being most frequent in occurrence, and most likely to be available on all the cases. In many instances, however, information on every item was not to be had, and the tabulations, for the most part, had to be made on the basis of fewer than 251 cases.

SECTION I — THE OFFENSES COMMITTED

The statistics concerning the various offenses committed by this group of adolescents have been divided into four major groups depending upon the type of offense. Those who were merely committed to Truant School were classified as *truants* those who in addition to Truant School commitment had appeared in the Children's Court on delinquency charges were classified as *delinquents,* those who in addition to truancy and delinquency, or who merely in addition to truancy, had appeared in the Magistrates Courts were classed as *misdemeanants,* and those who, regardless of other offenses, had appeared in the Court of General Sessions or had been charged with felonies were classed as *felons*. One exception to this classification must be noted. In several cases, boys who had been truant were later arraigned in the Magistrates Court for a single minor traffic violation. These few cases, because of the trivial nature of the misdemeanors, were allowed to remain in the truancy classification.

Table I
Present Age of All Offenders, by Groups

AGE	Total	Truants	Delinquents	Misdemeanants	Felons
14	1	1			
15	1	1			
16	2	1	1		
17	5	3	2		
18	8	2	6		
19	30	14	7	3	6
20	35	23	8	2	2
21	48	20	11	10	7
22	85	43	16	11	15
23	36	16	3	12	5
Total cases	251	124	54	38	35
Median, years	20.9	20.9	20.3	21.3	21.2

PRESENT AGE OF ALL OFFENDERS

The ages of the offenders were obtained from the school record cards on file at the Bureau of Attendance. Since the school usually requires proof of age through birth certificate, the ages given here can be regarded as generally authentic.

The comparison by age of the different groups is necessary in order that we should know whether we are dealing with groups of the same age or of different ages. If we are dealing with groups of different ages and if the groups committing the more serious offenses are considerably older than the other groups, then we cannot say whether the other groups will in time also commit serious offenses or not. If all of the groups, on the other hand, are of equal age then whatever differences in type of offense exist among them may be considered as true differences and the groups themselves as distinct in their normal responses to social situations.

Table I shows that the median * age for truants was 20.9 years, for delinquents 20.3 years, for misdemeanants 21.3 years, and for felons 21.2 years. The group who have committed only juvenile delinquencies, therefore, is on the average a full year younger than the group who committed misdemeanors and felonies. The group who have not been in difficulties at all, that is the truancy group, are on the average three months younger than the misdemeanants and felons. These figures would indicate that the boys who had

---

* The median has been used in most instances instead of the arithmetic mean, as being more representative of central tendencies of groups.

been charged with serious offenses were somewhat older than those in the delinquency group and approximately of an age with those in the truancy group. Thus, out of 251 cases, 197 or .78 were of the same approximate age. Of these, 124 were presumably adjusted and 73 were poorly adjusted. The remainder, 54 delinquency cases, were a year younger. The adjusted group, therefore, may be regarded as being truly different from the poorly adjusted group, in that both are of the same age but of altogether different type of career. The delinquency group, consisting of .27 of the cases, being a year younger, may during the coming year commit a number of more serious offenses, although this is somewhat problematical as over four years† have elapsed since they were in the Children's Court, during which time they have not been arraigned on any charges.

Table II
Birthplace of Parents

Country	Number	Proportion
Native born:		
United States	37	.15
Foreign born:		
Italy	141	.58
Russia	20	.08
Austria	18	.07
Ireland	15	.06
Hungary	3	.01
Germany	3	.01
Switzerland	3	.01
Spain	2*	
Bermuda	1*	
British West Indies	1*	
Czecho-Slovakia	1*	
China	1*	
Greece	1*	
Poland	1*	
Sweden	1*	
Unknown	2*	
Total cases	251	1.00

SEX, RACE AND NATIONALITY

The group of 251 cases consists of 248 boys and 3 girls. The race division is, White, 243; Negro, 7; Chinese, 1.

The birthplace of parents, shown in Table II, is given in .15 of the cases as native and in .85 as foreign-born. Italy leads with .58 of the foreign-born.

In order to test the accuracy of this sampling of cases an analysis was made of the land of birth of the parents of all truants committed in New York City, 1918 to 1922 inclusive. This group

---

† The age limit of the Children's Court in New York city is 16 years.
* Less than .01.

consisted of 4,476 cases. The nativity of parents in that group was as follows:

Country	Number	Proportion
United States	863	.19
No record	338	.08
Other countries	126	.03
Italy	2,270	.51
Ireland	286	.06
Russia	259	.06
Austria	138	.03
Germany	74	.01
Poland	62	.01
England	32*	
Hungary	18*	
Scotland	10*	
	4,476	1.00

The comparison of our sample of 251 cases with the total of five years' intake of the truant schools shows Italy holding the lead in both instances. The other countries vary slightly in their proportions, Russia .02, and Austria .04. This table, therefore shows that the group now being studied is racially a quite accurate sample of the total admissions to the Truant Schools over a period of five years.

TOTAL NUMBER OF ARRAIGNMENTS

This group of 251 adolescents have been arraigned before the Bureau of Attendance, the Children's Court, Magistrates and Criminal Courts, a total of 679 times, divided as follows: Truancy 377, delinquency 130, misdemeanors 117, and felonies 55.

Table III
Total of Arraignments, by Groups

	Total	Truants	Delinquents	Misdemeanants	Felons
Cases	251	124	54	38	35
Arraignments	679	179	161	165	174
Average number of arraignments		1.4	3	4.3	5

Table III shows that not only do the four groups differ in severity of their offenses but also in the number of their arraignments. The truants were arraigned for truancy on the average of 1.4 times, the delinquents were arraigned for combined truancy and delinquency on the average of three times per individual, the misdemeanants were arraigned for all offenses on the average of 4.3 per person and the felons an average of five times per person. In other words, increased seriousness of offense was accompanied by increased number of court arraignments.

* Less than .01.

Table IV
Proportion of Arraignments by Type of Offense

OFFENSE	TRUANTS			DELINQUENTS			MISDE-MEANANTS			FELONS		
	Cases	Arraignments	Average	Cases	Arraignments	Average	Cases	Arraignments	Average	Cases	Arraignments	Average
Truancy	124	179	1.4	54	85	1.6	38	60	1.6	35	53	1.5
Delinquency				54	76	1.4	38	21	.55	35	33	.94
Misdemeanor							38	84	2.2	35	33	.94
Felony										35	55	1.6

PROPORTION OF ARRAIGNMENTS BY TYPE OF OFFENSE

In Table III was indicated the total number of arraignments for each group. In table IV is shown the nature of the arraignments and their proportion among the different groups. It will be seen that there is no practical difference in the number of truancy commitments among the different groups, the average per individual ranging from 1.4 for the truancy group to 1.6 for the delinquent and misdemeanant groups. The number of delinquency arraignments is much more significant. The children whose delinquency career ended in the Children's Court appeared on the average of 1.4 times. The children who became misdemeanants, appeared on the average of .55 times, and those who became felons appeared .94 times. These figures indicate that the child who appears in the Children's Court more frequently is less likely to become a serious offender later, than if he appears less often. This would seem to be an indication of the efficacy of the Children's Court in stemming the tide of criminality. As for misdemeanors, the misdemeanant group committed on the average of 2.2 apiece whereas the felons committed only .94 apiece. The felons were arraigned on the average for felonies 1.6 times per person. The felons therefore tended to be arraigned for felonies almost twice as often as they were arraigned for misdemeanors.

DESCRIPTION OF OFFENSES

The legal description of charges in terms of Grand Larceny, Petit Larceny, etc., gives only a very formal picture of the difficulties that these young people have encountered in their process of growth. In order to give a more real picture of the type of things they have done, the various offenses committed by each individual have been classified according to not only the charge but the offense, which in many instances was given on the police record in concrete terms, such as "crap game" or "turning on fire hydrant in street." These tabulations have been given by groups in the following order: truants, delinquents, misdemeanants and felons. The offenses are given chronologically for each individual in the three latter groups. In this manner the delinquency history of each of the 251 cases has been made available.

TRUANTS

The 124 truants were committed a total of 179 times; 70 or .56 were committed once; 53 or .43 were committed twice, and one boy was committed three times. The three girls in the sampling of 251 cases were each committed once.

RECORD OF ARRAIGNMENTS FOR JUVENILE DELINQUENCY GROUP

Each offense represents a different child, except where offenses are bracketed, indicating successive arraignments

Year of birth	Date of arraignment	Charge	Offense	Disposition
1908	6- 9-16	Juvenile delinquency..	Stealing in company with other boys..............	Probation...........
1906	6-27-21	Juvenile delinquency..	Forced entrance to building and stole merchandise, value, $500.............	Probation...........
1906	10-21-16	Juvenile delinquency..	Attempt to steal lamp and blankets from wagon......	Probation...........
{ 1909	4- 7-23	Juvenile delinquency..	Disorderly conduct........	Suspended sentence...........
{ 1909	8-27-20	Juvenile delinquency..	Entered place and broke number of articles............	Probation...........
{ 1911	1-14-25	Juvenile delinquency..	Stole tools...............	Probation...........
{ 1911	10-27-25	Juvenile delinquency..	Broke show-case of drug store and stole safety razors....	Catholic Protectory............
1910	5- 9-19	Juvenile delinquency..	Stole pocketbook...........	Probation...........
1911	1- 3-19	Juvenile delinquency..	Stole machinery from apartment house..............	Probation...........
{ 1906	6-16-20	Juvenile delinquency..	Abusive language to mother.	Juvenile asylum..
{ 1906	6-16-20	Juvenile delinquency..	Ungovernable child........	Probation...........
{ 1906	6-25-20	Juvenile delinquency..	Violation of parole........	Juvenile asylum..
{ 1906	11-24-21	Juvenile delinquency..	Staying away from home....	Jewish Protectory
1906	1-28-20	Juvenile delinquency..	Forced entrance to store and stole groceries............	Probation...........
1909	3- 3-25	Juvenile delinquency..	Burglary, butcher shop.....	New York Catholic Protectory..
1907	7-19-21	Juvenile delinquency..	Stole a horse and wagon, value, $300.............	Probation...........
{ 1906	6- 7-16	Juvenile delinquency..	Stealing copper wire........	Probation...........
{ 1906	3-17-17	Juvenile delinquency..	Stealing oranges...........	Catholic Protectory............
1908	4- 9-20	Juvenile delinquency..	Incorrigible, ran away from home.................	Probation...........
1908	4- 7-23	Juvenile delinquency..	Burglary, broke open gas meter.................	Probation...........
1906	5-26-20	Juvenile delinquency..	Ran away from home, slept in hallway...............	Catholic Protectory............
1909	12- 1-22	Juvenile delinquency..	Running away from home...	Discharged........
1908	10-25-19	Juvenile delinquency..	Burglary..................	Discharged........
1908	3-29-19	Juvenile delinquency..	Stealing from store.........	Probation...........
1906	10- 2-18	Juvenile delinquency..	Burglary..................	Probation...........
1906	9- 7-18	Juvenile delinquency..	Attempted burglary........	Probation...........
1906	7-22-22	Juvenile delinquency..	Selling papers and annoying passengers...............	Discharged........
{ 1906	6- 2-17	Juvenile delinquency..	Entered flat and stole $27 and jewelry..............	Probation...........
{ 1906	6- 8-17	Juvenile delinquency..	Stole pigeons..............	House of Refuge..
1910	11-23-20	Juvenile delinquency..	Stole cheese, value $55.....	Sentence suspended...........
{ 1907	1-19-22	Juvenile delinquency..	Burglary..................	Sentence suspended...........
{ 1907	12-22-20	Juvenile delinquency..	Stole letter from letter-box containing money order...	No disposition...
1909	11- 7-19	Juvenile delinquency..	Stole horse and wagon......	Sentence suspended...........
1906	7-25-18	Juvenile delinquency..	Larceny of canvas bag containing auto repairs.......	Discharged........
1910	12-11-17	Juvenile delinquency..	Setting fire to papers in public school................	Probation...........
1907	12-22-19	Juvenile delinquency..	Stealing pocketbook, value $48....................	Discharged........
1910	10- 6-25	Juvenile delinquency..	Simple assault.............	Probation...........
1908	4-22-20	Juvenile delinquency..	Stole two boxes of crackers..	Probation...........
{ 1907	5- 6-16	Juvenile delinquency..	Stealing flowers from park...	Not held..........
{ 1907	11-12-19	Juvenile delinquency..	Breaking globe on lamp-post.	Probation...........
1910	5-16-26	Juvenile delinquency..	Burglary, loft.............	Probation...........
1906	11- 6-20	Juvenile delinquency..	Stole purse from coat pocket.	Probation...........

Record of Arraignments for Juvenile Delinquency Group — concluded

Each offense represents a different child, except where offenses are bracketed, indicating successive arraignments

Year of birth	Date of arraignment	Charge	Offense	Disposition	
1907	4-12-22	Juvenile delinquency..	Attempt to pass forged check for $20.................	Sentence suspended........	....
1906	12- 3-17	Juvenile delinquency..	Trespassing on railroad tracks	Discharged......	....
1910	9-23-21	Juvenile delinquency..	Grand larceny............	Catholic Protectory........	....
1906	5-19-21	Juvenile delinquency..	Cut complainant with pen knife..................	Discharged.....	....
{ 1906	1-26-20	Juvenile delinquency..	Stole clothing and jewelry, value $55.............	Probation..........	....
{ 1906	2-26-20	Juvenile delinquency..	Stole hat and coat from public school...............	Probation........	....
1909	3-18-25	Juvenile delinquency..	Burglary................	Discharged......	....
1912	1-29-24	Juvenile delinquency..	Burglary, forcing window and stealing chairs...........	No disposition...	....
1907	12-13-19	Juvenile delinquency..	Violation of parole.........	Discharged......	....
1907	6-30-19	Juvenile delinquency..	Trespassing on railroad tracks	$1 fine.........	....
1907	7-10-19	Juvenile delinquency.	Flying pigeons on roof......	Dismissed.......	....
	5-26-18	Juvenile delinquency..	Burglary................	Probation........	....
{ 1905					
{ 1905	11-10-19	Juvenile delinquency..	Entered through skylight and stole three pigeons........	Sentence suspended........	....
{ 1905	3-10-20	Juvenile delinquency..	Stealing box of apples, value $10...................	Jewish Protectory.	....
1906	9-24-19	Juvenile delinquency..	Ran away from home.......	Probation........	....
{ 1907	5-18-22	Juvenile delinquency..	Stole lamp from subway....	Sentence suspended........	....
{ 1907	5-24-23	Sentence suspended...	Loud and boisterous........	Discharged......	....
1909	4-13-22	Juvenile delinquency..	Taking package from wagon.	Catholic Protectory...........	....
1906	5-30-23	Juvenile delinquency..	Attempt to pick pocket.....	Catholic Protectory...........	....
1908	9-15-24	Juvenile delinquency..	Forcing entrance to grocery store and stealing $30.....	Jewish Protectory	....
1907	10-13-18	Juvenile delinquency..	Stealing.................	Probation........	....
1907	2-18-21	Juvenile delinquency..	Violation of parole.........	Discharged......	....
1909	10- 2-23	Juvenile delinquency..	Breaking windows in school.	Probation........	....
1909	19-23-25	Juvenile delinquency..	Threatened boy if he did not allow act of sodomy on him	?	....
{ 1906	3-16-20	Juvenile delinquency..	Violation of parole.........	Catholic Protectory...........	....
{ 1906	8- 9-22	Juvenile delinquency..	Incorrigible, staying away at night..................	Catholic Protectory...........	....
{ 1906	9-18-25	Juvenile delinquency..	Violation of parole.........	Catholic Protectory...........	....
{ 1907	3-30-22	Juvenile delinquency..	Violation of parole.........	Probation........	....
{ 1907	11- 2-22	Juvenile delinquency..	Incorrigible..............	Children's Village.	....
1905	8-16-19	Juvenile delinquency..	Robbery, stealing food-stuffs from grocery store........	Sentence suspended........	....
{ 1908	12-18-24	Juvenile delinquency..	Violation of parole.........	New York Catholic Protectory..	....
{ 1908	10-15-24	Juvenile delinquency..	Violation of parole.........	Probation........	....
{ 1908	2-26-24	Juvenile delinquency..	Incorrigible..............	Supervision, probation officer..	....
{ 1908	5-21-24	Juvenile delinquency..	Violation of parole.........	Probation........	....

RECORD OF ARRAIGNMENTS FOR MISDEMEANANT GROUP BY INDIVIDUAL CASES

Year of birth	Date of arraignment	Charge	Offense	Disposition	
1906	12-13-18	Juvenile delinquency..	Burglary................	Catholic Protectory...........	....
	1-20-25	Unlawful entry.......	Entered apartment house....	Penitentiary.....	....
1907	6- 1-22	Disorderly conduct...	Throwing missile from truck on passersby............	Sentence suspended........	....
1905	9- 7-27	Disorderly conduct...	?....................	Sentence suspended	....
1905	4-15-26	Disorderly conduct...	Crap game.............	Fined $1...........	....
1905	4- 2-15	Juvenile delinquency..	Trespassing............	Discharged.......	....
	3-14-17	Juvenile delinquency..	Larceny of watch, value $4.50	Probation........	....
	3- 9-22	Violation Education Law.............	Failed to attend school......	Sentence suspended........	....
	6-22-22	Violation Education Law.............	Failed to attend school......	Truant school....	....
	7-12-22	Disorderly conduct...	Turning on fire hydrant in street..................	Discharged.......	....
	4 -3-23	Assault, reduced to disorderly conduct....	....	3 months, work house..........	....
	9-27-23	Grand larceny, reduced to disorderly conduct	....	$10 fine...........	....
	12-31-23	?...................	Trespassing on Navy ground.	Discharged.......	....
	12-14-24	Disorderly conduct...	Fighting in street.........	$5 fine............	....
	12 -2-24	Disorderly conduct...	Abusive language..........	30 days, work house..........	....
1906	11-13-25	Violation traffic law..	Speeding.................	$25 fine...........	....
1906	3- 2-22	Juvenile delinquency..	Disorderly conduct.........	Probation.........	....
1907	9-22-22	Violation Corporation ordinance..........	Obstructing sidewalk with push-cart...............	Sentence suspended........	....
	7- 7-23	Violation Corporation ordinance..........	Peddler, no license.........	$10 fine or 10 days	....
1907	5-17-26	Volstead Act.........	Possession of wine.........	Discharged.......	....
1909	2- 2-26	....	Bookmaking.............	Discharged.......	....
1907	4-19-24	Disorderly conduct...	Shooting crap............	$1 fine............	....
1906	7-28-26	Violation traffic law...	Speed 40................	$25 fine...........	....
1905	4-30-20	Juvenile delinquency..	Associating with immoral persons..................	Discharged, sent to truant school	....
	3- 3-24	Violation traffic law...	Obstructing traffic.........	$3 fine............	....
	11-26-24	Violation traffic law...	Speed 27................	$25 fine...........	....
	5-15-25	Petit larceny.........	Stealing and breaking open slot machine............	Discharged.......	....
1909	9-25-24	Assault.............	Striking complainant on head	10 days, workhouse..........	....
1906	12-16-22	Disorderly conduct...	Stealing ride on street car...	Sentence suspended........	....
	12- 1-25	Disorderly conduct...	Cards..................	Discharged.......	....
	7-29-26	Violation traffic law...	Speed..................	$50 fine...........	....
	7-12-26	Violation traffic law...	Speed..................	$25 fine...........	....
1905	8 -1-22	Violation traffic law...	Passing street car on left...	$1 fine............	....
	11-10-22	Violation traffic law...	No name on wagon.........	Sentence suspended........	....
	12-14-22	Violation traffic law...	?.....................	$2 fine............	....
	6- 3-24	....	Obstructing sidewalk.......	$5 fine............	....
	10-27-24	Violation traffic law...	Speed 30................	$50 fine...........	....
	1- 9-25	Violation traffic law...	Obstructing view..........	$5 fine............	....
	3-31-25	Violation traffic law...	Restricted street..........	$4 fine............	....
	5-14-25	Violation traffic law...	Obstructing traffic.........	$5 fine............	....
1909	7- 9-25	Juvenile delinquency..	Stole package 7 cartons cigarettes.............	Sentence suspended........	....
	10- 1-25	Disorderly conduct...	Improper suggestion........	Probation.........	....
	12- 2-25	Disorderly conduct...	Forcing through turnstile....	Sentence suspended........	....
1907	3-22-25	Petit larceny.........	2 bottles of milk...........	Discharged.......	....
1907	5- 4-20	Juvenile delinquency..	Throwing bricks from roof...	Acquitted........	....
	4-12-22	Juvenile delinquency..	Robbing Chinese laundryman..................	Sentence suspended to complete truancy commitment...	.....

Record of Arraignments for Misdemeanant Group By Individual Cases—continued

Year of birth	Date of arraignment	Charge	Offense	Disposition
1907	9-21-24	Disorderly conduct	Shooting crap	Discharged
1905	6- 5-27	Disorderly conduct	Vagrancy	30 days, workhouse
	11- 9-27	Volstead Act	?	Pending
1907	4-28-25	Petit larceny	Stole sweater value $50	Sentence suspended
1906	5-11-18	Juvenile delinquency	Felonious assault	Sentence suspended
	11-12-24	Disorderly conduct	?	$2 fine
	9-10-25	Disorderly conduct	Crap game	Sentence suspended
1905	11-12-18	Juvenile delinquency	Violated probation	Discharged
	4-20-22	Violation Education Law		Sentence suspended
	5-25-22	Violation Education Law		Truant school
	7-22-22	Disorderly conduct	Crap game	Discharged
1906	2-12-18	Juvenile delinquency	Broke window and stole $50 worth of crackers	Paroled
	2-11-26	Disorderly conduct	Malicious mischief, broke window	Sentence suspended
1905	9-14-19	Juvenile delinquency	Stole from store	Probation
	3-30-20	Juvenile delinquency	Burglary	Probation
	11-14-22	Violation traffic law	Failed to stop on signal	$4 fine
	7-28-23	Disorderly conduct	Crap game	Sentence suspended
	10-26-23	Volstead law	Possession of 10 cases of whiskey	No disposition
	1- 7-24	Violation traffic law	No mirror	$2 fine
	4-30-24	Violation traffic law	Wrong side of street	$2 fine
	2-19-25	Violation traffic law	Restricted street	$2 fine
	2- 5-24	Violation traffic law	Improper turn	$2 fine
	1-29-27	Volstead law	?	Discharged
1905	3- 2-22	Disorderly conduct	Entering theatre thru exit	$2 fine
	1-21-25		No chauffeur's license	$25 fine
	6-19-25	Violation Corporation ordinance	No public cart license	$5 fine
	8- 5-25	Violation traffic law	Restricted street	$3 fine
	8-17-25	Violation traffic law	Failed to keep to right	$2 fine
	9-21-25	Violation traffic law	Speed 25	$25 fine
1906	12-23-23		No operator's license	$10 fine
1906	6-17-22	Petit larceny	Stealing electric bulbs	Sentence suspended
1905	5- 6-24	Violation traffic law	Restricted street	$3 fine
	5-19-25	Violation traffic law	Dense smoke	$5 fine
1905	5-20-16	Juvenile delinquency	Breaking window	Probation
	10-18-22	Violation Corporation ordinance	Driving advertising wagon, no permit	Sentence suspended
	8-27-24	Disorderly conduct	Sleeping on roof	$5 fine or 5 days
	9-15-24	Disorderly conduct	Annoying complainant	$10 fine or 10 days
1907	12-11-25	Disorderly conduct	Loitering in toilet	Sentence suspended
1907	7-15-24	Petit larceny	Stealing chestnuts value $15	Discharged
1908	11- 4-24	Disorderly conduct	Malicious mischief	No disposition
1908	5- 9-26	Disorderly conduct		10 days, workhouse
	9-20-26	Petit larceny	Stealing auto as a "lark"	Reformatory
1906	11- 3-21	Juvenile delinquency	Larceny of coat from auto	Probation
	1-21-22	Juvenile delinquency	Burglary; attempt to force door of grocery store	Probation
	11- 5-24	Disorderly conduct	Annoyance	$5 fine
	8- 4-25	Disorderly conduct	Violation of parole	House of Refuge
1905	2-14-19	Juvenile delinquency	Soliciting baggage	Discharged
	4-16-16	Juvenile delinquency	Begging on street	Catholic Protectory
	7- ?-25	?	Minor offense	Committed to jail for several weeks
1906	9-27-20	Juvenile delinquency	Remains away from home	Discharged
	5-13-26	Violated Corporation ordinance	No name and address on wagon	$3 fine

Record of Arraignment for Misdemeanant Group By Individual Cases—concluded

Year of birth	Date of arraignment	Charge	Offense	Disposition	
1906	10-19-26	Disorderly conduct...	Interfering with wagon......	?...............	....
	11- 1-26	Assault, 3rd degree...	....	Discharged......	....
	?	Disorderly conduct...	....	Sentence suspended........	....
1906	3-28-18	Juvenile delinquency..	Stole quantity of labels and fountain pens............	Catholic Protectory..........	....
	1-25-22	Juvenile delinquency..	Attempt to force entrance to apartments............	Catholic Protectory..........	....
	11- 2-22	Burglary (pleaded petit larceny)........	Tried to force rear door of tailor shop..............	New York City Reformatory...	....
1907	2- 7-25	Disorderly conduct...	Loitering with chisel (burglar's tools).............	House of Refuge..	....
	1925	None...............	Unprovoked assault upon an officer in an effort to escape House of Refuge.........	Transferred to Elmira Reformatory..........	....

RECORD OF ARRESTS FOR FELONY GROUP BY INDIVIDUAL CASES

Year of birth	Date of arraignment	Charge	Offense	Disposition
1906	4- 1-21	Burglary	Burglary of store	Penitentiary
	7-23-21	Grand larceny	Stole auto	Discharged
	2-25-23	Burglary	?	Probation, two years
1905	8-12-20		Maintaining live pigeons, no permit	Sentence suspended
	5-23-22	Disorderly conduct	Sodomy on 11 year old boy	New York City reformatory
	12-22-21	Violation Education law	Failed to attend school	Sentence suspended
	11- 7-24	Attempt grand larceny	Riding in stolen auto, also violation of parole	Sentence suspended and returned to Reformatory
1905	1- 8-21	Juvenile delinquency	Violation parole (probably theft)	Truant school, transferred to Catholic Protectory
	12-10-20	Grand larceny	Stole horse and wagon, value $430	Sentence suspended
1906	3-22-19	Juvenile delinquency	Forced entrance to flat	Catholic Protectory
	8- ?-26	Grand larceny	Stealing auto	Probation
1909	6-13-27	Rape	Attempt rape on an 8-year old girl	Reformatory
1907	8-20-20	Juvenile delinquency	Hitching on cars	No disposition
	11-23-26	Robbery	?	Discharged
1907	3-29-23	Disorderly conduct	?	Probation
	4- 3-23	Burglary	Entered flat	New York City Reformatory
	3-10-24	Unlawful entry	Attempted larceny	Discharged
	12- 5-24	Burglary	?	Sentence suspended
	3-26-24	Carrying concealed weapon	Carried revolver	Sentence suspended
	9-29-25	Burglary	Entered apartment	Penitentiary
1908	10-21-19	Juvenile delinquency	Stole keys and rubber stamps value $2	Probation
	10-27-26	Grand larceny	Stole $315	Reformatory
1906	3-26-15	Juvenile delinquency	Larceny	Probation
	5-16-20	Juvenile delinquency	Burglary	Catholic Protectory
	7-24-23	Disorderly conduct	Attempt to steal money	Discharged
	2-27-23	Burglary	Burglary of store	Discharged
	3-28-24	Robbery	At point of revolver stole $85	Discharged
1906	3-27-16	Juvenile delinquency	Stole candy	Probation
	6- 9-23	Burglary	Forced door and stole cigars, value $140	Discharged
1906	12-26-21	Juvenile delinquency	Burglary, bank book and $1.35	Sentence suspended
	8-18-25	Attempted felonious assault	Threw brick at officer	30 days, workhouse
	10- 9-26	Grand larceny	?	Discharged
	8- 6-24	Burglary	Store	New York City Reformatory
	3- 8-26	Disorderly conduct	Disorderly person	30 days, City Jail, Patterson, N. J.
1905	4- 5-22	Violation Education law		Truant school
	?	Violation Education law		Sentence suspended
	11- 7-22	Felonious assault		Discharged
1906	5-28-19	Juvenile delinquency	Throwing stones	Probation
	1-22-25		No chauffeur's license	2 days, workhouse
	6-27-25	Disorderly conduct	Crap game	$1 fine

31

Record of Arrests for Felony Group by Individual Cases—continued

Year of birth	Date of arraignment	Charge	Offense	Disposition	
1906	4-12-25	Felonious assault.....		Discharged......	....
	1-12-24	Volstead Act.........		Discharged......	....
1909	11- 4-20	Juvenile delinquency..	Burglary, forced window....	Probation........	....
	11- 9-25	Wayward minor......	Incorrigible, refuses to attend continuation school.......	Probation........	....
	2-23-26	Violation Education law.............	Failed to attend school......	Sentence suspended........	
	9-29-26	Disorderly conduct...	Impairing morals of minor...	House of Refuge..	....
	9-29-26	Grand larceny.......	Stole money from complainant's pocket, $17.........	New York City Reformatory...	....
1906	10-16-22	Rape...............		Suspended sentence...........	....
	3-16-25	Attempted burglary...	Forced window............	Discharged......	....
1909	8-11-16	Juvenile delinquency..	Destroying tent on playground................	Discharged......	....
	11-16-23	Juvenile delinquency..	Violation of parole.........	House of Refuge..	....
	6-17-24	Juvenile delinquency..	Fugitive from justice........	House of Refuge..	....
	10-11-26	Grand larceny.......	Stealing $2,512............	Napanoch Institute............	
1907	6-20-19	Juvenile delinquency..	Forcing skylight and stealing tools...................	Probation........	
	3-30-23	Burglary, 3rd degree..		Sentence suspended........	
	2-16-23	Burglary, 3rd degree..		Probation........	....
	5-7 -27	Homicide............	(auto)...................	Dismissed grand jury............	
1906	2-24-15	Juvenile delinquency..	Attended moving pictures alone..................	Discharged......	
	11-11-16	Juvenile delinquency..	Incorrigible...............	Probation........	
	10- 4-20	Petit larceny........		Discharged......	....
	10-18-22	Robbery............	Stole pin and money........	Sentence suspended........	
	4-10-23	Robbery............		Reformatory.....	
	2-18-26	Robbery............		Discharged......	
	2-23-26	Robbery............		Discharged......	
	3-22-26	Robbery............		Discharged......	
	6-21-26	Robbery............		Discharged......	
	8-22-26	Attempted robbery...		Discharged......	
1906	11- 1-19	Juvenile delinquency..	Escaped from training school.	Returned........	
	8-27-23	?..................	Possession of narcotics......	Reformatory.....	
	4-24-25	....	Violation of parole..........	Returned to Reformatory......	
	4-20-25	Robbery............	Cash and jewelry, value $650	Dismissed........	
1906	7-31-21	Juvenile delinquency..	Burglary.................	Discharged......	
	8-14-24	Disorderly conduct...	Crap game................	$2 fine..........	
	11-11-25	Burglary............	Stole quantity of leather....	Discharged......	
1906	5-3 -23	Robbery............	Robbed checks, $1,317 and $9,467..................	Discharged......	
1907	5-31-18	Juvenile delinquency..	Stole lead pipe from buildings	Probation........	
	12-17-18	Juvenile delinquency..	Petit larceny.............	Catholic Protectory...........	
	7-12-22	Juvenile delinquency..	Larceny of commercial auto.	Probation........	
	2-14-23	Juvenile delinquency..	Attempted robbery.........	House of Refuge..	
	5- 2-26	Robbery............	?.......................	Discharged......	
	7-20-26	Disorderly conduct...	Lush work................	4 months workhouse........	
	3-28-27	Attempted grand larceny, 2nd.........	Attacked man and attempted robbery................	Penitentiary.....	
1905	8- 8-20	Juvenile delinquency..	Possessing revolver.........	Probation........	
	6-25-21	Juvenile delinquency..	Violation parole...........	Probation........	
	5-14-22	Disorderly conduct...	Creating disturbance near home..................	Sentence suspended........	
	8-15-26	Disorderly conduct...	Loud language............	Sentence suspended........	
	6- 4-22	Violation Education law.............		Truant School....	
	8-24-26	Attempted robbery...	?.......................	Elmira Reformatory............	
1906	5- 5-25	Violation traffic law..	Improper turn............	$3 fine..........	
	10- ?-27	Grand larceny.......	Stealing tires from auto.....	Penitentiary.....	

Record of Arrests for Felony Group by Individual Cases—concluded

Year of birth	Date of arraignment	Charge	Offense	Disposition	
1906	8- 9-24	Disorderly conduct...	Shooting crap.............	Discharged......	....
	8-31-26	Grand larceny.......	?.......................	Sentence suspended........	....
1909	5-28-19	Juvenile delinquency..	Stole bottle of chili sauce from auto............	Discharged......	....
	12-19-21	Juvenile delinquency.	Broke window and stole $50.	Sentence suspended........	....
	? ? 22	Juvenile delinquency..	Stole shoes and jewelry.....	Catholic Protectory	
	? ? 26	Robbery 1st, grand larceny 2nd........	?.......................	Napanoch Institute.........	....
1909	12- 7-22	Juvenile delinquency..	Struck girl................	Catholic Protectory........	....
	1-18-25	Juvenile delinquency..	Breaking plate glass window.	Discharged......	....
	4- 9-25	Grand larceny.......	?.......................	New York State Reformatory...	....
	12-28-25	Grand larceny.......	Stole pocket-book.........	New York City Reformatory...	....
	1927	....	Escaped New York City Reformatory............	Sent to Elmira...	....
1906	5- 3-18	Juvenile delinquency..	Stealing goods, value $3.60...	Discharged......	....
	6- 4-18	Juvenile delinquency..	Stealing auto.............	Catholic Protectory............	
	11-24-22	Disorderly conduct...	Bad companions..........	Probation.......	....
	1-26-23	Disorderly conduct...	Violation of probation......	New York City Reformatory...	....
	9- 4-24	Disorderly conduct...	Violation of probation.......	Returned to penitentiary......	....
	11-16-25	Robbery............	?.......................	Dismissed by grand jury.....	....
	2-24-26	Robbery, 3rd degree...	?.......................	State prison, 5-10 years; transferred to Elmira	....
1905	3-17-19	Juvenile delinquency..	Burglary.................	Probation.......	....
	6- 9-26	Grand larceny.......	?.......................	Delivered to police, White Plains.........	....
1907	3- 4-24	Burglary............	Forced door of complainant.	Discharged.....	....
1909	8-11-24	Violation Corporation ordinance.........	Peddling without license....	$3 fine............	....
	? ? 26	Petit larceny.........	?.......................	2 years probation	....
	5-26-26	Burglary, 3rd........	Shoes, value $99..........	Elmira Reformatory............	
1907	11- 5-20	Juvenile delinquency..	Loitering.................	Discharged.....	....
	5-16-25	Disorderly conduct...	Obstructing sidewalk........	Discharged......	....
	6-30-27	?..................	Selling narcotics...........	Acquitted.......	....
1906	6-14-24	Disorderly conduct...	Crap game................	Sentence suspended........	....
	5-23-27	....	Violation of parole..........	Penitentiary.....	....
	1-25-25	Burglary............	?.......................	New York City Reformatory...	....
	12-26-26	Grand larceny.......	?.......................	Dismissed, grand jury.........	....

Table V
Nature of Juvenile Delinquencies, by Groups

	Delinquents		Misdemeanants		Felons	
Number of cases	54		38		35	
Number of arraignments	76*		21*		33*	
	No.	Prop.	No.	Prop.	No.	Prop.
Assault	2	.03	1	.05	1	.03
Robbery	5	.06	1	.05	1	.03
Burglary	18	.25	3	.14	7	.21
Unlawful entry	1	.01	1	.05	1	.03
Larceny	21	.28	6	.27	11	.34
Disorderly conduct	5	.06	3	.14	3	.09
Peddling and begging	1	.01	2	.10		
Ungovernable child	4	.05			1	.03
Disorderly child	6	.08	2	.10	3	.09
Truancy						
Violation Railroad Law	2	.03	1	.05	1	.03
Violation corporation ordinance	1	.01	1	.05		
Sex offenses	1	.01				
Unclassified					2	.06
Violation of probation	9	.12			2	.06

NATURE OF JUVENILE DELINQUENCIES

Table V gives a tentative answer to the question as to whether the type of delinquent act was different for the boys who eventually turned out to be felons than it was for the boys who subsequently were not felons. The table does not indicate any reliable difference for the three groups except that the misdemeanor group is somewhat low in the number of burglaries committed.

Table VI
Misdemeanors by Number and Type of Offense

	Misdemeanants	Felons
Number of cases	38	35
Number of arraignments	84	33
Offenses		
Disorderly conduct		
Burglary, reduced	1	0
Grand larceny, reduced	1	0
Felonious assault, reduced	1	0
Pushing and jostling	0	1
Throwing missile	1	0
Crap game	6	4
Turning on hydrant	1	0
Trespass	1	0
Street fight	1	1
Abusive language	1	0
Bookmaking	1	0
Stealing ride	2	0
Gambling	1	0
Improper suggestion to minor	1	0
Vagrancy	2	1
Malicious mischief	5	0
"Crashing theatre"	1	0
Loitering	1	0
Unclassified	7	7
Wayward minor	0	1
Violation education law	4	6
Violation corporation ordinance	6	3

Table VI—Continued

	Misdemeanants	Felons
Minor traffic violations	17	1
Speeding	7	0
Assault	2	0
Petit larceny	7	2
Unlawful entry	1	1
Impairing morals of minor	0	2
Burglary tools	1	0
Volstead Act	4	1
Narcotics	0	2

RECORD OF MISDEMEANORS

In table VI is recorded the different misdemeanors committed by the misdemeanant and felony groups. The misdemeanant group, it will be seen, is markedly different from the felony group with respect to number of offenses, despite their almost equal size.

An interesting side light on the occupation of the two groups is shown in the record of traffic violations. In 24 instances misdemeanants were fined for different traffic offenses. In only one instance was a felon fined. In other words, a fair proportion of the misdemeanant group earn a living as truck drivers and taxi chauffeurs but the felony group are not so occupied.

Table VII
Felonies by Type of Offense

Offense	Number of Arraignments	Proportion
Burglary	15	.27
Grand larceny	14	.25
Robbery	16	.29
Felonious assault	3	.05
Rape	2	.04
Narcotics sale	2	.04
Attempted grand larceny	1	.02
Concealed weapon	1	.02
Homicide	1	.02
Total	55	1.00

RECORD OF FELONIES

Table VII shows the type of felonies committed by the felon group. Burglary, grand larceny and robbery head the list and constitute .81 of all arraignments. These are not crimes of passion nor of the nature of fraud but are property offenses involving both stealth and violence, crimes typical of the young adult offender.

Table VIII
Arraignments and Convictions, by Groups

OFFENSE	TRUANTS		DELINQUENTS			MISDEMEANANTS			FELONS		
	Arrested	Convicted	Arrested	Convicted	Proportion	Arrested	Convicted	Proportion	Arrested	Convicted	Proportion
Truancy	179	179	85	85	....	60	60	....	53	53	.....
Delinquency	....	....	76	61	.80	21	15	.70	33	25	.76
Misdemeanor	....	....	....	....	....	*84	69	.82	33	27	.82
Felonies	....	....	....	....	....	....	....	....	†55	31	.56
Totals	179	179	161	146	....	165	144	....	174	136	.....

* 2 cases pending disposition.
† 1 case, disposition not known.

CONVICTIONS

In table VIII is shown the proportion of convictions in the different groups. The proportion is not given for the truancy commitments since in this group for every truancy arraignment there was a commitment. The general question raised by this table is whether those who became felons succeeded "in getting away with it" more than the other groups. The facts point in the negative. In the Children's Court the delinquent group were convicted in .80 of the cases, the misdemeants .70, and the felons .76. In the Magistrates Courts the misdemeanants and felons were convicted both .82 of the time. The number of convictions for felony offenses is much lower than for the others. This is probably characteristic of felony cases in general.

Table IX
Disposition of Cases, by Groups
TRUANTS
179 arraignments, all committed
DELINQUENTS

TYPE OF OFFENSE	Total arraignments	DISCHARGED		FINED		INSTITUTIONAL COMMITMENTS		PROBATION	
		Number	Proportion	Number	Proportion	Number	Proportion	Number	Proportion
Truancy	85	....	....	....	....	85	1.00	....	....
Delinquency	76	16	.21	1	.01	18	.24	41	.54

MISDEMEANANTS

Type of Offense	Total arraign-ments	Discharged		Fined		Institutional Commitments		Probation		Pending	
		Number	Proportion	Number	Proportion	Number	Proportion	Number	Proportion	Number	Proportion
Truancy	60	....	....	...	....	60	1.00	....	...	...	....
Delinquency	21	6	.29	....	....	4	.19	11	.52	...	....
Misdemeanors	84	13	.16	37	.44	15	.18	17	.20	2	.02

FELONS

Type of Offense	Total arraign-ments	Discharged		Fined		Institutional Commitments		Probation	
		Number	Proportion	Number	Proportion	Number	Proportion	Number	Proportion
Truancy	53	....	....	...	....	53	1.00	....	......
Delinquency	33	8	.24	....	....	11	.33	14	.43
Misdemeanors	*33	7	.21	4	.13	11	.33	11	.33
Felonies	†55	23	.42	....	....	22	.40	9	.18

* 1 Volstead Act violation, discharged; 3 narcotics sale, 1 discharged, 2 committed.
† 1 grand larceny, disposition not known.

DISPOSITION OF CASES

In table IX the disposition for offenses committed by the various groups are recorded. Here the question raised is whether the same type of punishment was accorded to all cases. The delinquency group were committed to institutions in .24 of the cases and placed on probation in .54. The misdemeanant group when arraigned in the Children's Court were committed in .19 of the cases and placed on probation in .52. The felons when in the Children's Court were committed to institutions in .33 of the cases and placed on probation in .43. The delinquents and misdemeanants had approximately the same proportion of probation treatment and the felony group had somewhat less, in the Children's Court. A considerably larger proportion of the felony group were committed to institutions than were members of the other two groups. For misdemeanors, the misdemeanant group were committed to institutions in .18 of the cases and the felony group in .33.

In general, the boys convicted of felony were more often discharged, less frequently fined, and more frequently committed to institutions, than the misdemeanant group, .44 of the misdemeanant group being punished by small fines. The felony group when tried for felony cases were committed to institutions in .40 of the cases, discharged in .42 and placed on probation in .18.

The general conclusion one may draw from this table is that the boys who ended up as felons had less opportunity for making good, through being placed on probation or fined, and were subjected to a greater amount of punishment by means of institutional commitment than were the other two groups. Whether the felony group would have become felons under different treatment this report does not presume to say but it can merely point out the type of treatment accorded and the final present day status of the group as criminals.

SPOT MAPS OF RESIDENCES OF CASES

Two spot maps, on pages 38 and 39, show the residences of the 251 children at the time of commitment to truant school in 1920–21. While the distribution of residences is borough-wide, it is confined very largely to areas of poor housing, which fringe the water-fronts or which border on commercial districts. The cluster of cases in the Upper East Side represents an area in which truancy is a grave problem, and in which the second largest number of juvenile delinquency cases in the Borough occur, according to the records of the Children's Court.

SECTION II — SOCIAL FACTORS

The following social factors are compared in this report, for the four groups of cases, ranging from those only truant to those arraigned for felonies: Nativity of parents, nativity of offender, recency of immigration of parents, size of family, position of client in sibling series, family income, income per person, employment of mother, civil status of home, number of rooms, congestion as measured by persons per room, degree and type of philanthropic aid given, and mobility.

Since the study was made, not upon a segregated group, but upon a group at large in the community, there was difficulty in obtaining complete data on all items. Therefore, not every one of the 13 social factors has data on all 251 cases, and on some items there is information on half of the group or less. The extent to which the accuracy of the report is affected by this unavoidable incompleteness, differs, of course, depending on the nature of the item. Discussion of the question of accuracy will accompany the statistical tables.

Table X
Nativity of Offenders and Parents

	Nativity of Fathers		Nativity of Mothers		Nativity of Offenders	
	No.	Proportion	No.	Proportion	No.	Proportion
Cases giving data	234	1.00	237	1.00	247	1.00
Native	30	.13	40	.17	202	.82
Foreign born	204	.87	197	.83	45	.18

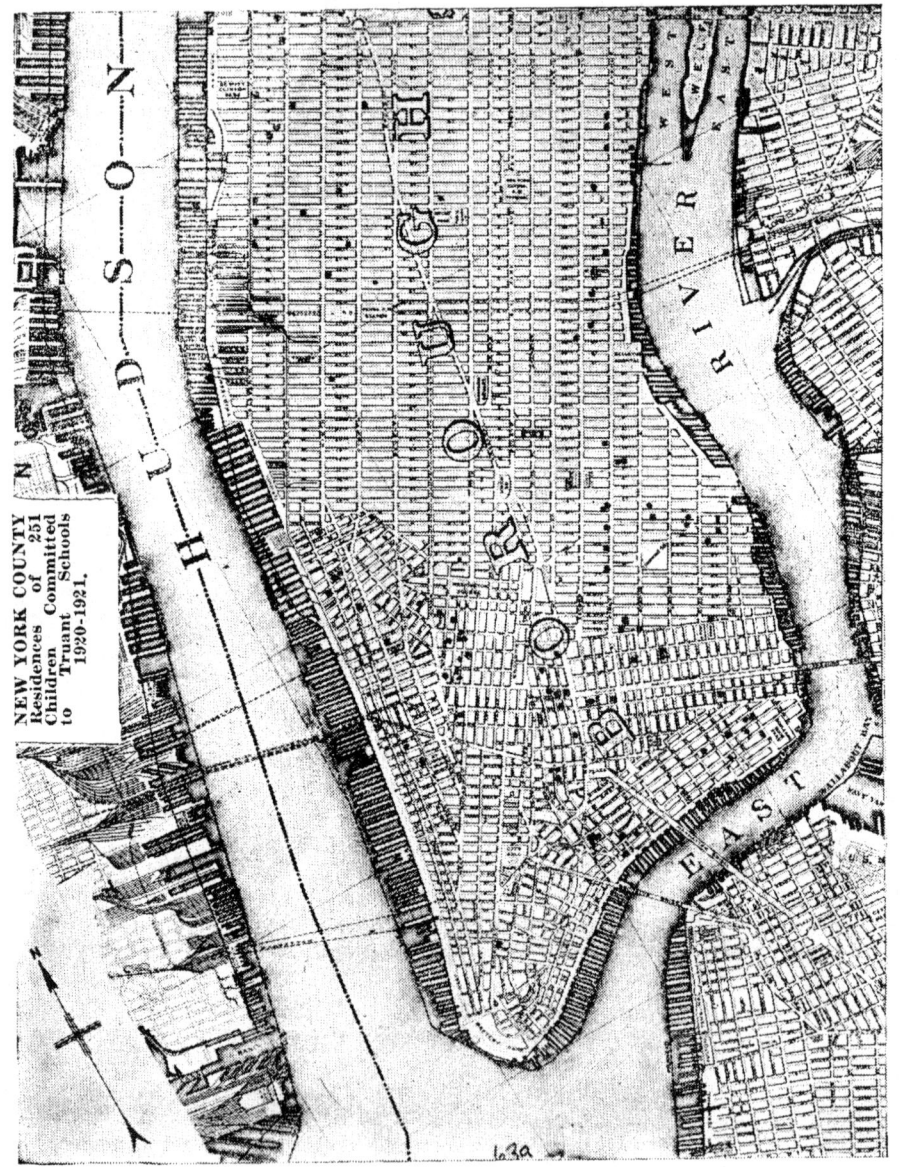

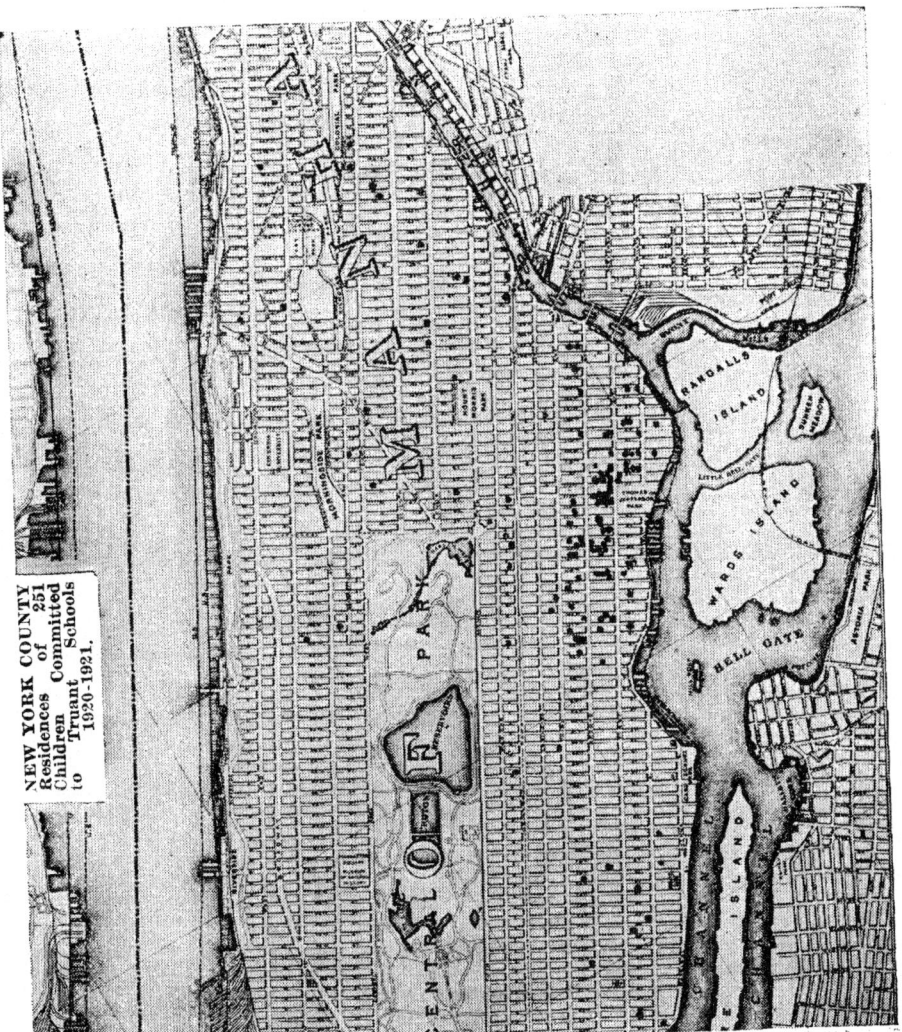

NEW YORK COUNTY
Residences of 251 Children Committed to Truant Schools 1920-1921.

Table XI
Nativity of Offenders and Parents, by Groups
NATIVITY OF FATHERS

	Truants		Delinquents		Misdemeanants		Felons	
	No.	Proportion	No.	Proportion	No.	Proportion	No.	Proportion
Cases giving data..	115		51		35		34	
Native	16	.14	7	.13	2	.06	5	.15
Foreign born	99	.86	44	.87	33	.94	29	.85

NATIVITY OF MOTHERS

	Truants		Delinquents		Misdemeanants		Felons	
	No.	Proportion	No.	Proportion	No.	Proportion	No.	Proportion
Cases giving data..	116		53		35		34	
Native	20	.17	10	.19	4	.11	6	.18
Foreign born	96	.83	43	.81	31	.89	28	.82

NATIVITY OF OFFENDERS THEMSELVES

	Truants		Delinquents		Misdemeanants		Felons	
	No.	Proportion	No.	Proportion	No.	Proportion	No.	Proportion
Cases giving data..	123		53		37		35	
Native	97	.79	42	.79	33	.89	31	.89
Foreign born	26	.21	11	.21	4	.11	4	.11

NATIVITY OF OFFENDERS AND PARENTS

The figures for the whole group show that the parents were predominantly foreign-born and the offenders predominantly native born. Whether this has any sociological significance, depends upon the makeup of the population from which the group was drawn. The population of Manhattan Borough, New York City, determined by the Federal Census in 1920, approximately the time at which these cases were committed as truants, was as follows:

Table XII
Nativity of Males and Females, In Manhattan, 1920

	MALES, OVER 21		FEMALES, OVER 21		MALES, UNDER 21	
	No.	Proportion	No.	Proportion	No.	Proportion
Native	271,178	.39	295,542	.42	338,902	.88
Foreign born	423,541	.61	403,879	.58	44,965	.12

A comparison of Table X and Table XII shows the proportion of foreign born in the whole adult population to be greater than native, but the disparity is not so great as in the 251 cases studied.

The foreign born parents were approximately 25% more numerous in the group studied than foreign born adults in the total borough population.

Foreign born offenders were .06 more numerous in the group studied than were foreign born children in general in the 1920 population of Manhattan Borough.

The composition of the group of cases studied is more foreign than the composition of the general population but the excess of foreign-born parents is four times as great as the excess of foreign-born offenders. The conclusion, therefore, must be that foreign parentage is a significant factor among those favoring persistent truancy, or worse.

A comparison of Tables X and XI, shows a tendency for foreign parentage to increase as the severity of offenses increase, except for the felony group, among whom foreign parentage is less than among the other groups. The offenders themselves, as seen in Table X and XI, are of approximately the same proportion of native and foreign as in the general population, in the truancy and juvenile delinquency group, but the proportion of foreign-born offenders is cut in half in the misdemeanant and felony section.

A rough inverse proportion appears to exist, therefore, in the parent-child relation for offenses of misdemeanor degree. As offenses of greater severity than truancy and juvenile delinquency are committed, the proportion of foreign parents rises and of foreign children drops. For felonies, the proportion of foreign-born parents and foreign-born children are both reduced.

The question arises as to how accurate a sample of the entire truant group is the present group of 251 with regard to nativity. To answer this, the nativity statistics on parents of all children committed to Truant School in the five Boroughs of New York City, 1918–22 inclusive, were obtained from the Bureau of Attendance. Of a total of 4,476 cases the parents in 686 instances or .19 of the total, were native. In the sample of 251, .17 of the mothers and .13 of the fathers were native. The average of these figures is within .04 that for the 4,476 cases. The sample of 251 cases can therefore be considered accurate, in representing the proportion of native and foreign parents in the truancy group as a whole.

Table XIII
Recency of Immigration Among Parents of Offenders

Time of Arrival	Total				Truant				Delinquent				Misdemeanor				Felony			
	Father		Mother		Father		Mother		Father		Mother		Father		Mother		Father		Mother	
	Number	Proportion	Number	Proportion	Number	Proportion	Number	Proportion	Number	Proportion	Number	Proportion	Number	Proportion	Number	Proportion	Number	Proportion	Number	Proportion
Before 1900	69	.32	60	.32	37	.43	29	.32	11	.26	12	.28	11	.38	7	.23	10	.42	12	.48
In 1900	10	.06	8	.04	7	.08	4	.04	2	.04	2	.06			2	.07	1	.04		
After 1900	103	.62	120	.64	42	.49	58	.64	30	.70	28	.66	18	.62	21	.70	13	.54	13	.52

RECENCY OF ARRIVAL OF PARENTS

Table XIII shows the time at which the foreign born parents came to the United States. This data is recorded for 182 out of 204 foreign born fathers and 188 out of 197 foreign born mothers. Since 234 of the 251 offenders were born between 1904 and 1908, it is clear that parents arriving after 1900 would be in general, still old-world in their customs and attitudes, during the early youth of their off-spring. This arbitrary date was therefore set, to divide recent from more remote immigration, in an attempt to measure recency of immigration as a factor in crime.*

This table shows that approximately one-third of the parents were of the older immigration and two-thirds were of the newer immigration. Unfortunately, no comparison can be made between the figures on the sample of 251 cases and the figures for Manhattan as a whole, since the Federal census does not provide information on the length of residence of the foreign-born. The proportion of new and older immigrant parents remain the same for all groups of offenders until the felons are reached. Here half of the parents are of the older immigration. These facts, taken in connection with those on nativity, suggest that felonies in this group have been committed more, in proportion, by sons of persons acquainted with the ways of the land than by those of recent arrivals, whereas minor infractions of the law are more likely to have been committed by sons of more recent immigrants.

---

* The phrase "recency of immigration" has no connotation here, other than the number of years intervening between the arrival of the parents and the birth of the offender. The particular time at which this group of families arrived was of course determined by the median age of the group studied. Had an older group of offenders been studied, most of the parents would have come before 1900, but the number of years elapsing between immigration and birth of the offender would have remained the same.

Table XIV
Number of Children in Family in Relation to Type of Offense

Number of Children	Truancy	Delinquency	Misdemeanor	Felony	Total
1	8	2	1	1	12
2	13	5	3	3	24
3	15	7	5	2	29
4	22	6	4	6	38
5	18	8	4	5	35
6	11	22	5	5	43
7	16	5	8	4	33
8	5	3	3	3	14
9	10	1	1	4	16
10	1		1		2
11	2	1	1	1	5
Total of cases	121	60	36	34	251
Median	4.2	5.1	5.2	5	

NUMBER OF CHILDREN IN RELATION TO TYPE OF OFFENSE

Table XIV shows no marked association between number of children in family and type of offense, but differentiates to a degree between offenders and non-offenders. Thus delinquents, misdemeanants and felons were from families having 5 to 5.2 children, whereas truants were from families having an average of only 4.2 children.

Table XV
Family Position of Offender

Position of Offender	Truant		Delinquent		Misdemeanant		Felon	
	Number	Proportion	Number	Proportion	Number	Proportion	Number	Proportion
First child	30	.24	10	.18	8	.21	5	.14
Second child	25	.20	15	.28	14	.37	11	.31
Intermediate child	46	.37	21	.39	11	.29	15	.43
Next to last child	6	.05			2	.06		
Last child	17	.14	8	.15	3	.07	4	.12
Total of cases	124		54		38		35	
Median size of family	5		6		6		5	

POSITION OF CLIENT IN RELATIONSHIP TO OFFENSES

In Table XV, the relation of the position of the client in the family, to degree of misconduct, is considered. The oldest and second oldest children are more likely to be offenders than either the youngest or the next youngest. The child least likely to be an offender is the next youngest. The second child has the worst record for delinquency, misdemeanors and felonies.

These findings, in association with those on the number of children in comparison with degree of misconduct, are somewhat disturbing to set notions of crime causation. Not alone does the size of the family have little influence on type of career, but the children who were most anti-social were the earlier ones, at a time when the family was small.

In view of the fact that two-thirds of the first and second children were the sons of newly arrived immigrants, an explanation of their predisposition to crime would have to be in terms of the differences between their experiences and those of their younger sisters and brothers. In the absence of definite facts, the following possibilities may be considered:

1. The parents, through ignorance of ways that are both new and urban, are less able to follow the behavior of their earlier than of their later off-spring.

2. The parents, because of economic insecurity, are less able to provide means of amusement for their earlier off-spring.

3. The first children, because of this economic pressure, are forced at an earlier age to become wage-earners, and when through incompetence, sloth, or desire for pleasure, they are idle, the parent-child conflict is greater than for the younger children.

The tendency toward misconduct of the youngest child cannot be explained on any of the above grounds. Whole volumes have been written on the psychology of the last child. It is popularly supposed that the last child is most indulged, and that, if true, would present an interesting parallel to the least-indulged oldest children.

The real factors that are responsible for the situation disclosed in these statistics, are of course not known, and it remains for further research to uncover them.

Table XVI
Income in Relation to Type of Offense

INCOME	Total	Truants	Delinquents	Misdemeanants	Felons
$10	11	5	2	2	2
15	8	6		1	1
20	29	17	6	2	4
25	28	14	6	4	4
30	30	10	10	8	2
35	30	13	7	6	4
40	30	12	9	3	6
45	15	7	3	2	3
50	15	7	3	2	3
Over $50	31	16	6	5	4
Number of cases	227	107	52	35	33
Median	$31	$31	$32	$30	$35

Table XVII
Income Per Person in Relation to Type of Offense

INCOME	Total	Truants	Delinquents	Misdemeanants	Felons
$2	22	13	2	3	4
3	28	11	4	10	3
4	41	21	11	3	6
5	29	7	11	8	3
6	33	22	6	2	3
7	13		5	5	3
8	26	11	5	3	7
10	9	4	1	2	2
12	9	5	2	1	1
14	6	2	3		1
Number of cases	216	96	50	37	33
Median	$4	$4.5	$4.7	$4.3	$5

INCOME IN RELATION TO TYPE OF OFFENSE

Tables XVI and XVII disclose no association between income and type of offense. Delinquents, misdemeanors and felons all come from families having the same average income. Nor does income differentiate offenders from non-offenders, for truants come from families of the same average income.

But all groups come from the lowest income class in the population. Criminality of all degrees in this group is 30 times as great as in the population at large, if we accept the estimate that one per cent of the population engage in crime. Therefore, the conclusion might be that poverty has a direct relation to crime in general, if not to type of crime.

This does not mean, however, that mere economic privation caused people to supplement their inadequate lawful incomes by ill-gotten gains. Such an explanation disregards the fact that many poverty-stricken groups have improved their status through wholly legal means, such as through the formation of labor unions, for example. Such an explanation disregards the fact that a portion of the economically depressed group in this study did not become criminal.

A more acceptable explanation is that this group of cases consists, on the one hand, of immigrants who have low incomes because of lack of opportunity, but who are morally sound, and on the other hand of family groups for whom poverty is merely an effect of such factors as lack of intelligence, plan-lessness, improvidence and idleness. Among this latter group, criminality must be traced to such complex factors as habit, family and neighborhood attitudes, rationalizations, effect of companionship and leadership, conflict with authority, etc.

Table XVIII
Occupation of Mother

OCCUPATION	Total	TRUANT		DELINQUENT		MISDE-MEANANT		FELON	
		Number	Proportion	Number	Proportion	Number	Proportion	Number	Proportion
Housewife	102	43	.50	31	.60	14	.50	14	.54
Home industry	37	12	.15	8	.15	8	.28	9	.34
Outside work	52	30	.35	13	.25	6	.22	3	.12
Number of cases.	191	85		52		28		26	

OCCUPATION OF MOTHERS

Table XVIII shows that .47 of all the mothers in this group of cases have been employed, either at tasks taking them outside of the home into shops, offices and factories, or at tasks occupying home time, such as clothing finishing, flower-making and acting as janitress.

The proportion of working mothers is almost the same for all four conduct groups, but the proportion of mothers who work away from home decreases, and the proportion of home-industry workers increases, with the increase in seriousness of the offenses committed. This seems contrary to common sense, and there is no satisfactory explanation for the figures. It may be, however, that mothers working away from home make more definite provision for the supervision of their children during working hours than do mothers who merely add work to home duties.

Table XIX
Civil Status of Home

FATHER	TOTAL		TRUANT		DELINQUENT		MISDE-MEANANT		FELON	
	Number	Proportion	Number	Proportion	Number	Proportion	Number	Proportion	Number	Proportion
Living with family	147	.65	73	.64	36	.70	19	.54	19	.73
Dead	53	.23	27	.24	9	.17	11	.30	6	.23
Away from family	26	.12	14	.12	6	.13	5	.16	1	.04
Number of cases	226		114		51		35		26	
MOTHER										
Living with family	193	.83	93	.80	46	.90	31	.90	23	.82
Dead	30	.13	21	.19	3	.06	2	.05	4	.14
Away from family	8	.04	3	.01	2	.04	2	.05	1	.04
Number of cases	231		117		51		35		28	

CIVIL STATUS OF HOME

In Table XIX the status of the family is considered for both parents, from three points of view: either the parent is living with the family, is dead, or is away from the family. The third classification includes desertions and separations. It will be seen that the father is living with the family in .65 of the cases and the mother in .83. This tendency of the mother to be the surviving parent in charge of the family persists throughout the tabulations. Thus, among the truant group the mother is present in .80 and the father in only .64; in the delinquency group the mother in .90 and the father in .70; in the misdemeanant group, the mother in .90 and the father in only .54; and in the felon group, the mother in .82 and the father in .73. Fewest mothers are living with the families in the truancy group. Here, .80 live with the family, .19 are dead, and .01 are away. Fewest fathers are at home in the misdemeanant group. Here, .54 are at home, .30 are dead, and .16 are away from home. The other figures do not seem to have special significance. It would seem then that the status of the home has a special importance in the truant and misdemeanant groups, the absence of the mother being disproportionately great in the truant group, and the absence of the father being disproportionately great in the misdemeanant group. In the felony group the family status appears, strangely enough, to be somewhat better than in certain other of the groups. Thus, the proportion of fathers living with the families is greater than in any other group, and the proportion of mothers living with the families is practically the same as that for the total group studied. The proportion of fathers away from the family is only one-third as high as for the group as a whole.

While an explanation for this latter fact is not easy to give, yet it may be pointed out that the facts themselves are in agreement with those in previous tables given on the relationship of degree of anti-social conduct to the period of residence of the parent. It was there shown that the boys committing felonies tended to be sons of parents acquainted with the habits of the land rather than sons of recently arrived immigrants. Misdemeanors then would seem to arise more in families of recent immigration where home conditions are somewhat disrupted through death or absence of the father, whereas felonies seem to arise in greater proportion among relatively better assimilated families and native families of less impaired civil status. This would indicate that the search for factors in serious crimes would have to go much further and deeper than would be brought to light in a sociological study of civil status of the home.

In general the numbers of parents living with the family is greater in this study than is indicated in the findings of other recent studies. Bonser, in a comparative study of delinquent and non-delinquent school children, found that the father was dead in .20 of the cases of delinquent boys, .63 of the delinquent girls, .06

among school boys and .05 among the school girls in the normal population.

Parsons quotes Shideler's estimate, that 25 per cent of all children in the United States live in homes broken by death, desertion, separation or divorce, but that the studies of the various groups of delinquents in this study, show that .40 to .70 of them come from such broken homes.

Bonser's study would indicate that the death of the bread winner affected the conduct of girls rather than boys.

Breckenridge and Abbott have also concluded that the loss of the father is more serious than the loss of the mother. Shideler has reached the opposite conclusion as has Sutherland. Our own figures indicate, as stated above, a greater proportion of fathers absent from the home in these cases, than of mothers.

Table XX
Size of Dwelling

Number of rooms	Total	Truants	Delinquents	Misdemeanants	Felons
2	15	8	5	2	0
3	43	12	13	10	8
4	42	16	16	5	5
5	27	10	4	7	6
6	7	3	1	1	2
7	1	0	0	1	0
Number of cases	135	49	39	26	21
Median	3.25	3.3	3.1	3.5	3.5

Table XXI
Degree of Housing Congestion

Persons per room	Total	Truants	Delinquents	Misdemeanants	Felons
1.0	9	3	2	4	0
1.2	19	8	4	5	2
1.4	15	3	7	1	4
1.6	12	2	6	2	2
1.8	18	9	3	2	4
2.0	12	6	3	3	0
2.2	11	3	3	3	2
2.4	1	1	0	0	0
2.6	6	1	1	2	2
2.8	1	1	0	0	0
3.0	9	2	3	2	2
3.2	1	1	0	0	0
3.4	3	2	1	0	0
3.6	2	0	1	0	1
3.8	0	0	0	0	0
4.0	2	0	1	1	0
Number of cases	121	42	35	25	19
Median	1.7	1.7	1.6	1.7	1.7

HOUSING CONGESTION

Table XX shows no association between the size of the dwelling and the degree of criminality but brings out the fact that all of the members of this group live in decidedly congested quarters, the median number of rooms ranging from 3.1 to 3.5 per family.

Table XXI which measures degree of housing congestion in terms of the size of the family in comparison with the size of the living quarters, also shows no such relationship, the median number of persons per room ranging from 1.6 to 1.7. In general, however, the entire group of cases came from areas of poor housing. Reference to the map showing the residences of the offenders brings out that point clearly to those familiar with housing conditions on Manhattan Island.

The degree of housing congestion among these 251 cases appears to be greater, however, than among the population in general in similarly congested areas. The State Board of Housing in its 1927 report quotes on page 45, a table showing the average number of persons per apartment in eight congested blocks on the Island of Manhattan. The average number of persons in the three room apartments was 2.86, in the four room apartments 3.82, and in the five room apartments 4.12. The average number of persons per room is .95 in the three room apartments, .95 in the four room apartments, and .82 in the five room apartments. Compared with these figures are those in Table XXI showing a median number of persons per room among the cases here studied of 1.7. In other words in the cases studied housing congestion is practically twice as great as in congested areas generally. Not only is congestion great but there is over-crowding even within the minimum standards set by the Commission of Housing and Regional Planning, which allows two persons to live in a two room apartment, four in a three room apartment, six in a four room apartment, and eight in a five room apartment.

It can be said therefore, that while the degree of criminality does not seem to be affected by the degree of congestion nevertheless this entire group of cases live under conditions of greater congestion than do the average poor. Congestion, therefore, would seem to have some association with truancy if not with more serious delinquency since all of these cases were at least truant.

Table XXII
Number of Social Service Agencies Registered on Families

No. of registrations.	None	1	2	3	4	5	6	7	8	9	10
No. of cases	63	54	45	29	19	9	6	4	0	1	1

Median 2.8 registrations.

Table XXIII
Type of Agencies Registered on Families

Type	Number of Registrations
Financial	155
Medical	117
Employment	16
Recreational	20
Child guidance	99
Foster care	14
Legal	14
Total	435

Table XXIV
Philanthropic Services Rendered

Type of aid	Total Aid	Truant	Delinquent	Misdemeanant	Felon
Financial	72	33	20	12	7
Medical	80	38	17	13	12
Child Guidance	*31	19	6	1	5
Employment	17	5	6	4	2
Recreation	15	3	9	2	1
Foster Care	7	4	1	2	0
Legal	5	1	0	3	1
Total Aid	227	103	59	37	28
Total cases aided	188	114	· 33	21	20
Average number of agencies per family	1.2	.90	1.8	1.8	1.4

* 65 additional cases were known to Probation Department of the Children's Court.

PHILANTHROPIC SERVICES RENDERED

Tables XXII and XXIII have been tabulated directly from the reports made by the confidential Social Service Exchange and represent all of the registrations. Seventy-five per cent or 188 cases were known to social service agencies, .25 or 63 cases were not known. A total of 435 separate registrations were made on 188 cases or an average of 2.3 agencies per family registered upon. The numerical order of registrations was: Financial 155, medical 117, child guidance 99, recreation 20, employment 16, foster care 14, legal 14. The economic status of the group is indicated by its large appeal for financial assistance. The gratifying large appeal for medical assistance, on the other hand is indicative of the tremendous community resources that exist for medical aid. Very significant is the small number of registrations by recreational organizations.

Table XXIV, philanthropic services rendered, has been compiled from the reports of social service agencies to the Sub-Commission on Causes. Of the 435 registrations there are reports on 227, somewhat over .50. The difference among the groups is not great and philanthropic aid, as far as quantity is concerned, may be regarded as almost a constant factor. More attention was given to families whose sons were juvenile and adult offenders than to those whose sons were only truant. These figures, of course, are inadequate in one sense, since they give no picture of the period over which aid was given. One may generalize by stating that the group received a great deal of philanthropic aid, chiefly financial and medical with negligible attention paid to recreation and employment.

Table XXV
Mobility

Number of times family moved	Total	Truant	Delin-quent	Misde-meanant	Felon
0	11	4	6	0	1
1	47	22	9	11	5
2	45	21	10	5	9
3	23	11	7	2	3
4	19	8	4	3	4
5	15	6	3	2	4
6	6	4	0	2	0
7	2	2	0	0	0
8	0	0	0	0	0
9	2	1	0	1	0
Total times moved	425	206	81	70	68
Total of cases	170	79	39	26	26
Average number of times moved	2.5	2.6	2.1	2.7	2.6

MOBILITY

The matter of mobility may seem somewhat unrelated to the problem of crime but upon reflection it will be seen that it does bear a good deal of relationship to the environmental factors in delinquency. Thus, the influence of a street gang is likely to be stronger over boys who live in a given neighborhood for long periods of time compared to those who move about a good deal.

The data for Table XXV were taken from the duplicate of the offender's school record, giving all home addresses from the time he entered school until his commitment to the Truant School in 1920 or 1921. Where families moved subsequent to this period the changed addresses were added to the total. This is, of course, not strictly accurate because there may have intervened changes of addresses between the one given in 1921 and the latest one known since. The data available on 170 families show that this group moved 425 times or an average of 2.5 changes of address per family. The comparative data for the four groups show that families of truants, misdemeanants and felons tended to move slightly more often than families of juvenile delinquents. The difference, however, is not considered large enough to be of any especial significance.

The question remains open however, as to whether this whole group has moved more or less than the average family of the same economic status. Comparative data would be difficult to find, particularly for the period since 1920 when the housing emergency in Manhattan and the resulting emergency rent laws reduced considerably the number of changes of residence.

Table XXVI
Police Record for Others in Family

	Total	Truant	Delinquent	Misdemeanant	Felon
Father	45	20	10	7	8
Mother	20	6	4	8	2
Sister	9	4	1	3	1
Brother	122	45	22	25	30
Total	196	75	37	43	41

Table XXVII
Extent of Criminal Record Among Families of Offenders

Group	Cases	No criminal record	Cases having criminal record	Proportion	Total arraignments	No. per case
Truant	124	70	54	.43	110	2.0
Delinquent	54	27	27	.50	67	2.5
Misdemeanor	38	13	25	.66	86	3.4
Felony	35	6	29	.83	79	2.7
Total	251					

GROUP	NUMBER OF DELINQUENCIES		NUMBER OF MISDEMEANORS		NUMBER OF FELONIES		Total Arrests
	Arrests	Proportion	Arrests	Proportion	Arrests	Proportion	
Truant group	21	.20	*62	.56	27	.24	110
Delinquent group	14	.20	†44	.65	9	.15	67
Misdemeanor group	12	.14	‡63	.73	11	.13	86
Felony group	16	.20	§39	.50	24	.30	79

* 26 additional cases of minor traffic violation.
† 19 additional cases of minor traffic violation.
‡ 26 additional cases of minor traffic violation.
§ 10 additional cases of minor traffic violation.

Table XXVIII
Arraignments Among Members of Families of Truants

	Father	Mother	Sister	Brother	Total
Juvenile delinquency			1	20	21
Misdemeanors:					
Wayward minor				1	1
Violation Education law	4	2		1	7
Volstead law	1				1
Non-support	1				1
Violation Corporation ordinance	2	4		8	14
Gambling	1				1
Disorderly conduct	4		1	11	16
Indecent performance				1	1
Narcotics				1	1
Traffic law	3			16	19
Speeding	1			4	5
Burglary tools				1	1
Attempted extortion				2	2
Petit larceny			1	2	3
Bigamy	1				1
Assault	5			2	7
Felonies:					
Grand larceny	1			6	7
Felonious assault				1	1
Robbery				1	1
Concealed weapon				2	2
Burglary				7	7
Sex offense	1			4	5
Homicide			1	2	3
Escaping prison				1	1
Total					129

Table XXIX
Arraignments Among Members of Families of Delinquents

	Father	Mother	Sister	Brother	Total
Juvenile delinquency			1	14	15
Misdemeanors:					
Wayward minor					
Violation Education law	4	1		1	6
Volstead law				2	2
Violation Corporation ordinance	5	2		2	9
Disorderly conduct	7			5	12
Traffic law	12			7	19
Narcotics				1	1
Speeding					
Petit larceny					
Assault	1			1	2
Felonies:					
Grand larceny				3	3
Robbery				2	2
Burglary				1	1
Sex offense					
Homicide	1	1		1	3
Total					75

Table XXX
Arraignments Among Members of Family of Misdemeanants

	Father	Mother	Sister	Brother	Total
Juvenile delinquency				12	12
Misdemeanors:					
Wayward minor					
Violation Education law	6	2			8
Intoxication	2			2	4
Violation Corporation ordinance	6	6	1	1	14
Disorderly conduct	5	1		10	16
Traffic law	6			20	26
Speeding	4			5	9
Unlawful entry				2	2
Petit larceny	1			1	2
Assault	3			5	8
Felonies:					
Grand larceny		1			1
Concealed weapon		1		1	2
Robbery				1	1
Burglary				4	4
Sex offense				1	1
Homicide	2				2
Total					112

Table XXXI
Arraignments Among Members of Families of Felons

	Father	Mother	Sister	Brother	Total
Juvenile delinquency				16	16
Misdemeanors:					
Wayward minor					
Violation Education law	1	2			3
Volstead Act	1				1
Non-support	1				1
Violation Corporation ordinance	1			5	6
Disorderly conduct	2			11	13
Trespass				1	1
Narcotics				1	1
Traffic law				10	10
Speeding				2	2
Unlawful entry				2	2
Petit larceny				5	5
Assault	1			4	5
Felonies:					
Grand larceny				4	4
Robbery				3	3
Burglary				16	16
Sex offense				1	1
Total					90

POLICE RECORD FOR OTHERS IN FAMILY

The numerical disproportion of fathers and brothers over mothers and sisters in numbers of arraignments merely follows the usual course of crime statistics in which the male sex is always predominant. Percentages have not been given for the four groups, as calculations would have to be on the basis of number of individuals comprising the families of each group, and this would more or less duplicate Table XXVII. The general tendency, however, was for the fathers, mothers and brothers to be offenders in greater proportion among the more serious than among the milder offenders. This will be more clearly seen in Table XXVII.

EXTENT OF CRIMINAL RECORD AMONG FAMILIES OF OFFENDERS

A remarkable relationship between the severity of the offenses committed by the former truant and the degree of criminality in the home background is shown in this table. Members of families of truants have criminal records in .43 instances; those of juvenile delinquents in .50 instances; those of misdemeanants in .66 instances; and those of felons, in .83 instances. These figures are perhaps among the most significant in the entire report. They reveal the close relationship of adequate home life with lawful behavior and of inadequate home life with unlawful behavior. They show that the children studied in this report were not merely subject to vicious external environment, but that in too many instances the very source of their moral training was defective.

On the other hand, no clear-cut relation is seen between type of offense committed by the children and those committed by other members, although the tendency among the felons is for the other members of the family to commit felonies likewise.

SECTION III—BEHAVIOR FACTORS

In the preceding section a number of social factors that are popularly supposed to affect conduct have received statistical analysis. In this section a group of behavior factors will receive consideration. This group of factors is gathered from behavior data on the offenders. That is, it represents their responses to the environment analyzed in part in the preceding section. These behavior factors are:—Onset of truancy, school conduct ratings, proficiency ratings, grades reached, gang affiliation, and vocational history.

Table XXXII
Onset of Truancy

Grade	Total	Truants	Delinquents	Misdemeanants	Felons
1	45	20	18	3	4
2	48	22	12	5	9
3	41	22	7	8	4
4	28	14	4	5	5
5	23	10	4	5	4
6	10	4	2	2	2
7	5	3	1	1	
8	1		1		
Continuation school	14	7	1	2	4
Cases	215	102	50	31	32
Median grade		3A	2A	3B	3B

Table XXXIII
Relative Amount of Truancy

CASES	Total	Truants	Delinquents	Misdemeanants	Felons
Cases	215	102	50	31	32
Days truant	28,231	13,486	6,964	3,574	4,207
Average per case	131	132	139	115	131

ONSET OF TRUANCY

Table XXXII tells the story of when truancy began. The date of onset was measured in the following manner: The school record for each child containing the chronological list of grades attended and number of absences per grade was analyzed and the four grades in which the child was most absent were recorded. The greatest absence was, of course, in the grade immediately preceding the commitment to Truant School. This method of selection eliminated all grades in which there was only a small amount of truancy. The results based on this method indicate, therefore, not when truancy began but rather when truancy became serious.

The data recorded on 215 cases show that truancy among this group of offenders began early in their school history, in the first grade in 45 instances, in the second grade in 48 instances, in the third grade in 41 instances and in the fourth grade in 28 instances. The 36 remaining cases were distributed between the fifth and eighth grades. Fourteen cases arose in Continuation School. On the majority of this latter group there was unfortunately not always available the early truancy record. The average grade at which truancy became serious ranged between 2-A and 3-B. Truants who became juvenile delinquents became serious truancy problems earlier than any of the other groups, commencing in 2-A. Truants who had no subsequent delinqency history became serious problems, on the average, a year later in grade 3-A. The average period of beginning serious truancy for the misdemeanor and felony groups was in grade 3-B.

While the above statistics do not indicate that the period at which truancy began was different for the 4 groups of cases it does show clearly that the entire group became maladjusted to their school surroundings at a very early period in their school history and that preventive work could have been initiated when the children were of an age to profit most from guidance.

Table XXXIII analyzes the relative amount of truancy among the different groups of offenders. The data for this table was obtained by adding the four outstanding term absences for each child and taking the average for each group. The results, contrary to expectations, do not show that the misdemeanants and felons were more truant than the others. The general average is 131 days of absence, the felons have a record of 131 and the misdemeanants have a record of 115. On the basis of Tables XXXII and XXXIII therefore, one may say that there could have been no prognosis of mild or serious misconduct either in terms of the degree of truancy or its time of onset.

Table XXXIV
School Conduct Ratings

MEDIANS OF GRADES GIVEN	TOTAL		TRUANT		DELINQUENT		MISDE-MEANANT		FELON	
	No.	Prop.	No.	Prop.	No.	Prop.	No.	Prop.	No.	Prop.
A	21	.10	12	.12	6	.12	1	.05	2	.10
B	160	.78	77	.77	39	.78	24	.82	20	.74
C	24	.12	10	.11	5	.10	4	.13	5	.16
Cases	205	....	99	....	50	....	29	....	27	....

SCHOOL CONDUCT RATINGS

In table XXXIV is taken up the question of the value of school marks as indications of future delinquency career. The data for this table consisted of all the term conduct marks received by offenders from the time they entered the first grade until the time of their truancy commitment in 1920 or 1921. The median was obtained for each child and it is these medians that are represented in the figures of the table.

The figures, based on 205 cases, show that in all of the four conduct groups "B" was the most frequent rating given. The "A" rating was received on the average, by .10 of the pupils. The felony cases received .10 of the "A's," the truancy and delinquency .12, while the misdemeanors had the poorest showing with .05. The average number of "B's" received was .78; the misdemeanor cases received .82, truancy and delinquency .77 and .78, and felony .74. "C" ratings were received on the average by .12 of the pupils. The group ratings were: Truancy .11, delinquency .10, misdemeanor .13, and felony .16.

According to these figures the misdemeanor group had somewhat less than its proper proportion of the better marks and the felony group had slightly more than its proper proportion of the worst marks. The differences, however, were not great enough to have any real significance. These statistics do not show that school ratings given by teachers are a real appraisal of the personality of the child.

Table XXXV
School Proficiency Ratings

MEDIANS	TOTAL		TRUANT		DELINQUENT		MISDE-MEANANT		FELON	
	No.	Prop.	No.	Prop.	No.	Prop.	No.	Prop.	No.	Prop.
A	2	.01	1	.01	1	.02	....	....	....	....
B	155	.75	79	.80	38	.76	17	.59	21	.78
C	47	.23	18	.18	11	.22	12	.41	6	.22
D	1	.005	1	.01	....	....	....	....	....	....
Cases	205	....	99	....	50	....	29	....	27	....

SCHOOL PROFICIENCY RATINGS

The ratings in school subjects shown in Table XXXV do not distinguish between future truants, delinquents and felons. The misdemeanant group, however, are decidedly poorer in academic work, having twice as many "C" ratings as the other groups. The fact that the misdemeanor group tend to be sons of recent immigrants may be one explanation of this.

Table XXXVI
Grade Reached

GRADE	Total	Truant	Delinquent	Misdemeanant	Felon
1					
2					
3	1		1		
4	1		1		
5	12	6		5	1
6	37	17	9	7	4
7	78	45	15	7	11
8	21	8	6	5	2
9	4	2	2		
High school	4	2	2		
Ungraded	1	1			
Total	159	81	36	24	18
Median grade		6.4	6.5	6	6.3

GRADE REACHED

Table XXXVI shows that the median grade reached ranged between 6-A and 6-B. There was no differentiation between the four groups on the basis of this tabulation.

Table XXXVII
Gang Affiliation

	Total	Truants	Delinquents	Misdemeanants	Felons
Number of cases	251	124	54	38	35
Gang member	54	15	22	10	7
Proportion	.22	.12	.40	.26	.20

GANG AFFILIATION

Table XXXVII showing gang affiliation of the four different groups is based upon data obtained in a variety of ways. Some of it is based on Children's Court reports, some on reports from social welfare agencies, and some from reports of police and court officers. The figures show that 54 out of the 251 cases were known to be members of gangs at some time in their career. Delinquents had the highest number, having 22 out of 54 or .40 thus designated. The felons had .20 and the misdemeanants .26 in gang groups. Only .12 of the truants associated in gangs. The chief significance of this table lies in the low proportion of gang affiliation among the truant group. However, the number of cases reported on is small and the results cannot be taken too authoritatively. It is significant that in the cases not reported on as being gang members there was no information as to whether gang affiliation had existed or not, therefore the number reported on is not by any means to be considered as the total of those who were in gangs, but merely as the total upon whom information was obtained.

Table XXXVIII
Degree of Skill in Position Held

	TOTAL		TRUANT		DELINQUENT		MISDEMEANANT		FELON	
	No.	Prop.	No.	Prop.	No.	Prop.	No.	Prop.	No.	Prop.
Cases	87	....	37	....	26	....	12	....	12	....
Jobs held:										
Unskilled	62	.50	21	.51	19	.29	11	.65	12	.57
Semi-skilled	47	.37	18	.44	15	.33	6	.35	7	.33
Skilled	17	.13	2	.05	13	.38	....	....	2	.10
Total jobs	126	....	41	....	47	....	17	....	21	....

DEGREE OF SKILL IN POSITION HELD

Although general employment information was available on more than half of the group of cases, only in 87 cases were the statements on jobs specific enough to classify them by type. The employment data for these cases was obtained in part from court and social service records and the remainder was secured from the records of the Continuation schools, through the courtesy of the director of the department.

The classification of the State Department of Labor was used in separating jobs into the three categories of skilled, semi-skilled and unskilled. This classification is based on the length of time necessary to learn a job, and on the general education necessary for it. Unskilled jobs are those requiring slight education, and can be learned on the average, in a week's time. Semi-skilled occupations either call for some education or experience or both, and are learned in periods varying from a month to a year. Skilled occupations include the usual trades, and require at least three years to learn. Apprentices in skilled trades are classed as skilled labor, on the basis of the end in view, rather than on their degree of training.

The statistics on this group show that a negligible number were skilled workers, except in the juvenile delinquency group, and that unskilled work was done by over half the cases in all groups except that of juvenile delinquents. No significant differences can be traced for the truants, misdemeanants and felons, because of the small number of jobs studied. The figures for the juvenile delinquents were enough different to merit separate attention. To the extent that these figures are indicative of general tendencies, it would seem that boys who have been only juvenile delinquents tend to enter better occupations than the other groups. The only obvious explanation is that the juvenile delinquents, as part of their court supervision, had their attention directed to good jobs, more than did the other groups, in their casual vocational experience.

Table XXXIX
Type of Job Held

Type of job	Total	Truant	Delinquent	Misdemeanant	Felon
Skilled					
Baker	2		1		1
Plasterer	2		1		1
Silver plater	1		1		
Book binder	1		1		
Barber	4		4		
Plumber's helper	2	2			
Butcher's helper	4		4		
Florist's helper	1		1		
Semi-Skilled					
Truck driver	18	9	4	2	3
Bus driver	1		1		
Taxi chauffeur	1	1			
Teamster	1	1			
Trucking	1	1			
Laundry driver	5		5		
Milkman	1	1			
Conductor	1	1			
Shipping clerk	1	1			
Auto mechanic's helper	2	1			1
Presser	1		1		
Piano varnisher	1		1		
Clerk in market	5	2	2	1	
Shoe clerk	1				1
Waiter	1				1
Elevator operator	1				1
Glass beveler	1			1	
Packer	1			1	
Farm hand	1		1		
Factory worker	3	3			
Bartender in speakeasy	1			1	
Unskilled					
Errands	27	12	10	2	3
Truck helper	11	2	2	4	3
Porter	2	1			1
Peddler	3	1		1	1
Bootblack	2	1			1
Office boy	2		1	1	
Laborer	12		6	3	3
Bootlegger	1	1			

TYPE OF JOB HELD

Table XXXIX tabulates the different jobs held under the three classifications. Outdoor work was favored over indoor work, two to one, there being 39 indoor and 86 outdoor jobs listed.

TABULATION OF JOBS BY CASES

In the following pages are shown the different jobs held by the members of the four groups, giving an idea of the tendency to diversity, wage range, and period of employment.

Truants—Vocational History of Client

CASE NO.	Year	Job held	Employer	Salary	Duration
1			Biscuit company.		
2		Helper on autos			
3	1926	Truckman	Auto factory. Self		Continuing.
4		Messenger	Institution	$14 per week. $40 per month and maintenance	
5			Trucking company		
			Book company		
		Truck driver	Trucking company		
6	1926	Laborer	Fruit company. Building contractor	$9 per day	2 years.
7		Driver	Trucking company		
8		Errand boy	Button company		
		Errand boy	Chain grocery store		
9					Unsteady.
10		Helper	Plumber	$18 per week	
		Delivery boy	Market	$30 per week	3 months.
11		Helper	Plumber	$17.50 per week	
		Driver			
12		Bootlegging			Short time.
		Worker	Battery factory	$20 per week	6 months.
13		Peddler	Fruits		
14		Worker	Silk factory	$13 per week	2 weeks.
		Messenger	Telephone company		Few days.
15				$12 per week	
16	1927	Driver	Trucking company		
17		No information			
18		Worked irregularly			
19	1927	Helper	Express company	$10 per week	
20	1921		Shoe store	$8 per week	
21	1920	Delivery man	Laundry	$15 per week	
22				$12 per week	
23		Telegraph messenger			Few months.
		Errand boy	Store		1 week.
		Errand boy	Parish house		
		Chauffeur, several other jobs, cab driver, etc	Chemical house		
24	1923	Helper on wagon	Trucking		
25		Conductor		$4.50 per day	?.
		Shipping clerk	?		
26	1926	Milkman		$35 per week	
27	1924	Truck driver		$19 per week	
28		Chauffeur	Ice cream concern	?	
		?	Manufacturer of chemicals		
29	1927		Poultry market	$30 per week	
30	1919	Chauffeur			Until government took it over.
31	1924	Errand boy	Truckman	$12 per week	
32	1924	Sold fish		?	
33		Bootblack			After school.
	1926	Takes care of horse and wagon for past 6 years, irregularly, receives about $10 per week			
34		Irregularly as chauffeur or fruit peddler		?	
35		Machine work in box factory			
36	1922	Errand boy	Printer	?	
37	?	?		?	
38	?	?	Cap factory	?	

Juvenile Delinquents—Vocational History of Client

CASE NO.	Year	Job held	Employer	Salary	Duration
1	1922	Helper	Beet company	?	Vacation.
2	1921	?	Worked in building with mother	$8 per week	?
3	?	Truck driver	?	?	Irregular.
4	?	Delivery boy	Brother-in-law, butcher. Is now learning trade	$20 per week	
5	?	?	Trucking company	?	Past 2 years.
6	?	?	Works in country for a relative	?	
7	?	Helper	Hospital	$10 per week	2 weeks.
8		Messenger	Button works	$10 per week	5 weeks.
9	1924	?	Laundry	$15 per week	?
10	1925	Driver	?	?	?
11	1925	?	Laundry	?	?
12	1926	Delivery boy	?	$40 per week	?
13	1927	Driver	Laundry	?	
14	1927		Baker	$32 per week	Present.
15			Works irregularly as a silver-work plater, since out of school	?	?
16	?	Varnisher	Piano company	?	?
17		Presser	Tailor	?	?
18		Snow laborer		?	?
19		?	Gas company	?	?
20		Works irregularly			
21	1927	Plasterer		$4 per day	Present.
22	1924	Delivery boy	Grocer	$12 per week	?
23	?	Bookbinder		?	?
24	1924	Standman	Fruiterer	$18 per week	?
25	1923	Worked steadily	?	?	?
26			Worked for Post Office Department during Christmas rush, shifting mail sacks		?
27	1924	Helper	Florist	$10 per week	?
28	?	Errand boy	?		After school.
29	?	Helper	Wet wash laundry, wagon	?	?
30	?	Errand boy	Bakery	?	?
31	?	?	Worked for uncle	?	?
32	?	Errand boy	Trimming company	$10 per week	1½ months.
33		Helper		$12 per week	1 week.
34	1924	?	Butcher	$10 per week	?
35	1927	?	?	?	?
36	?	Errand boy	?	$8 per week	?
37	?	?	Hat company	?	?
38		?	Candy factory	$8 per week	5 months.
39		Barber	42d street	$6.50 per week	?
40		Barber	102d street	$14 per week	?
41		Barber	97th street	$14 per week	?
42		Barber	103d street	$20 per week	?
43	?	Barber	For uncle	$20 per week	Present.
44	?	Selling vegetables	For father	?	?
45	?	Errand boy	?	?	?
46	1927	Office boy	Color company	$9 per week	4 months.
47	1927	Chauffeur	Fur storage	?	6 months.
48		Chauffeur	Bus	$35 per week	4 months.
49	1922	Chauffeur	Lumber company	$25 per week	?
50	1922	Driving soda water wagon	Worked with father in scale business	$13.50 per week $12 per week	4 days.
51	1922	Driving wagon		$15 per week	?

Misdemeanants—Vocational History of Client

CASE NO.	Year	Job held	Employer	Salary	Duration
1	?	?	Worked irregularly in grocery store and terminal	?	?
2	1924	?	Varnish company	$18 per week	3 months.
3	1924	?	Canning company	40 cents per hour	7 months.
4	1923	?	Woolen mills	$25 per week	4 months.
5	1922	?	Grocer	$6 per week	?
6	?	?	Paint shop	$10 per week	?
7	?	?	Wholesale grocers	$12 per week	?
8	1921	Office boy	?	$12 per week	2 weeks.
9	?	?	Not known	?	3 days.
10	1922	Messenger	Factory	$12 per week	2 months.
11	1923	?	Box factory	$16 per week	1 month.
12	1923	Loading and unloading truck	?	$10 per week	?
13	1922	Deck hand	?	?	?
14	1923	Peddler	?	?	?
15	1926	?	?	$10 per week	?
16	1922	Helper	Trucking	$14 per week	6 months.
17	1922	Beveler	Plate glass company	$12 per week	3 weeks.
18	1923	Laborer	Wet wash laundry	$3 per day	1 month.
19	1923	Helper	Trucking	$14 per week	?
20	1927	Truck driver	?	$30 per week	Present.
21	?	Does not work steadily. Tends bar in speakeasys			
22	?	Packer	Toys	?	?
23	?	Errand boy	Hat shop	?	?
24	?	Helper	Trucking	$25 to $30, two or three days work	irregular.
25	1925	Helper	Express	?	?
26	1925	Chauffeur		?	?
27	1922	?	Laundry	?	?
28	?	?	Department store	?	?
29	1927	Fruit stand		?	?
30	1922	?	Moving picture theatre	$7 per week	?
31	1922	Helper	Railroad	$16 per week	?
32	1923	Joined navy			
33	1927	?	Sweets and wafer company	?	?
34	?	Messenger	Telegraph company	?	?
35	?	Selling newspapers	News-stand	?	?
36	?	Flag boy	Railroad	?	?
37	?	Engraving	?	?	?
38	?	Stock boy	?	?	?
39	?	Errand boy		$12 per week	7 months.
40	?	Messenger	?	$12 per week	Few months.
41	?	Night helper	Garage	$22 per week	?
42	?	?	Riding Academy	?	?
43	?	Irregularly on truck and also shoveled snow			

Felony—Vocational History of Client

CASE NO.	Year	Job held	Employer	Salary	Duration
1	1920	Clerk	Shoe company	$15 per week	8 months.
2	1921		Printer	$12 per week	3 months.
3	1924	Waiter	In Boston	?.″	1 month.
4	1924		I. R. T. (Odd jobs since 1924)	?	Several weeks.
5		Truck driver		$18 per week	4 weeks.
6		Truck driver		?	?
7	1921	Bootblack	Barber shop	$5 to $6 per week	?
8	?	Errand boy	?	?	?
9		Errand boy	Candy store	$3 per week	After school.
10	?	?	Biscuit company	?	2 weeks.
11	1923		Trucking company	$5 per day	3 or 4 days a week.
12	1924	Cleaner	Barber shop	$10 per week	?
13	1926	Helper on Truck		$15 per week	?
		Peddler	?	?	?
14		Helper	?	?	?
15		Errand boy	?	?	?
16		Laborer	?	?	?
17		Elevator runner	?	?	?
18	1927	Helper	Mineral Water Co.	$25 per week	2 weeks.
19	1927	?	?	$7 per day	1 week.
20		?	Bakery	$25 per week	1 year.
21	1921	Clerk, checking valuables	Athletic club	$15 per week	Few months.
22		Helper	Auto mechanic	$10 per week	?
23	1925	Plasterer	For father	$66 per week	?

CASE HISTORIES OF FORTY-FIVE ADOLESCENTS

One-fifth of the group of 251 adolescents, consisting of every fifth case, chosen in consecutive order, have been given as intensive study as time permitted. Every possible source was utilized in securing a present-day picture of these cases. A mass of material was available at the outset, consisting of police card index records, finger-print records, Bureau of Attendance and grammar school data, and many reports from social service agencies.

These sources were supplemented in several ways. Every agency that had ever made contact with the family, but whose summary of contact had not been received, was visited and an abstract was made of their records. City Parole Commission and Court of General Sessions Probation Department records were studied and summarized. Correspondence with penal institutions and reformatories brought additional records. The Bureau of Criminal Identification of the New York Police Department gave valuable assistance by making discreet inquiries as to the known criminal activities of these cases. Finally, an effort was made to reach each client at his home.

This was not always possible. The last known address was frequently several years old, and families had to be traced from one address to another. This meant tedious work and many visits by the field investigators. Often, the family was not at home. Again, a single visit often did not suffice to gain the desired information, or the client himself was not at home, and return visits had to be made. Because of these difficulties, only 45 out of the 50 records are chronicled, and not all of the clients were interviewed.

Surprising candor characterized most of the interviews. In several instances, where the boy was known to be in bad company, or serving a jail sentence, the parents were euphemistic in their description of his present behavior. But, on the whole, the statements that were given either tallied with data obtained through other sources or stood on their own merit as being plain stories, unembroidered by fancy.

The cases have been divided into two groups—those who have been without a serious police record, and those who have had recent criminal records.

The group as a whole paints a colorful picture, but a discouraging one. Few of the so-called "adjusted" group deserve that title even though they are not delinquents. Social problems of every sort loom up, and one almost forgets that most of these youths are a bare half dozen years away from boyhood, so enmeshed are they in the vicissitudes and hindrances of their social heritages.

The case data itself is in many instances far too meager. Despite the fact that many social agencies served the families, the boys themselves were not often recognized as being serious problems and were usually dealt with only incidentally. They were merely on the fringe of the family problem and are described only in vague terms. Where the boys themselves were given attention the data available is painfully illustrative of the weakness of average case methods of half a dozen years ago, or even more recent years. The record is often but a bare statement of offenses, failures at meeting conditions of probation or parole, and jobs held. Where the records are loquacious, they are usually condemnatory, the side of the story representing the point of view of the boy himself being nearly always absent. One almost forgets that one is dealing with youngsters, whom, under other circumstances would have appealed to us as human and perhaps likeable.

To the extent, therefore, that these case histories must depend entirely upon materials that were gathered at times when these boys were in conflict with their surroundings, they are subject to prejudice. Since the records were not given free interpretation, but the facts were strictly adhered to, this was unavoidable. Only in the discussion that follows the individual cases has there been any opportunity for an evaluation of the facts presented.

Perhaps most lacking in the available case data, and therefore most worthy of attention, was data on the motives animating the delinquent behavior, and material descriptive of the social world occupied by these boys. Their interests, ambitions, loves, hates, grudges, prejudices—anything that would give a picture of the events culminating in disaster, was usually absent. Their play life, friends, hang-outs, group interests and attitudes, and status among companions—in a word, that portion of their personality peculiarly their own, free from the restriction of home and school—is but hinted at.

Until case methods are so generally proficient that illuminating data of the type sadly lacking here, are the basis of contact with offenders, little progress in treatment of individuals will be made.

ADJUSTED GROUP

Case No. 1—John R.,* age 17, arrested and sent to the Catholic Protectory in 1925, for participating in a series of petty store burglaries, has since been paroled and has worked steadily for two years for a trucking company. He married in October, 1927.

The parents were born in Austria and came to the United States in 1903. The father died in 1921. His history is not known and there is no police record for him.

The mother, age 45, is in good health and has remarried. The step-father has suffered a paralytic stroke, necessitating outside employment as a scrubwoman on the part of the mother.

The family has lived for many years in a fairly good neighborhood, occupying 4 comfortably furnished, clean rooms for which they paid $36 rental in 1925. They now live in the Bronx.

There were 3 children, 2 boys and a girl. The girl died when young. The older boy, born in 1905, is an elevator operator earning $18 a week. He has no police record.

John's developmental history is not known. His health as a boy was poor. He suffered from hernia and had swollen glands. His leg was injured in an automobile accident.

The detective bureau reports in their confidential investigation, that when he was a boy, he lived in a disreputable East Side neighborhood, where he met bad companions. "He was allowed to roam the streets at will, his parents having no control over him at all. He would stay out all hours of the night and steal anything he could get his hands on. These youthful thefts were usually disposed of at junk shops."

His school record was poor. He was retarded 5 terms before reaching grade 3B. He reached grade 7A at 15 years. His conduct was C and D and his work B and C. Truancy began in the first grade, and when he reached 2A and 2B, he was absent more than 50 days each term. He smoked, stole, talked obscenely, and bullied other children. He did not attend church.

He was first committed to the Truant School in 1920 at the age of 10, for 6 months. In April, 1921 he was recommitted and remained nearly a year, until March, 1922. He then returned to school, where he remained until 1925.

In that year, he was twice implicated in thefts. The first occasion was in January, 1925, when he was accused, with others, of stealing tools valued at $300 from a tinsmith shop. He was placed on probation in the Children's Court. In May, he was found with other boys at 1:30 in the morning, in the act of breaking a showcase in front of a store, and stealing safety razors. He admitted par-

---
* Fictitious names are used throughout.

ticipation in at least 4 other attempts at burglary in the past 3 months, and was committed to the Catholic Protectory. The police report that petty burglaries in his neighborhood ceased for a time when he was sent away.

He was paroled in October, 1925 and sent back to school, but he played truant, and worked without an employment certificate. He was returned and again paroled in November, 1926. He disappeared shortly thereafter and the Protectory officials to whom he is still on parole, have lost sight of him. They suspect that the mother knows his whereabouts, but is shielding him.

The police report, however, that he married in October, 1927, lives in the Bronx, and has worked steadily for a trucking company since his release. He is thought to be weak-willed and easily led and his associates are still not of the best. At the time of his marriage, 3 of his friends, who were present, left his home while the party was in progress, held up a man at the point of a revolver, and stole his car. They were caught and sentenced to Sing Sing. John, however, is believed to be "going straight" since his marriage.

Discussion: Unfavorable neighborhood and vicious companionship, lack of maternal supervision and incapacity for academic work led to this boy's difficulties. Why was not something done about it at a time when re-training was simple? Probably because the routine of "treatment" through Truant School committment was working so automatically that no one ever stopped to think of alternative methods.

But if no question was raised then, one should be raised now. How is it that the procedure of sending 10 year old children to disciplinary institutions, a procedure borrowed from the criminal courts, has ever been sanctioned, much less approved, among a group of educators?

Case No. 2—Pasquale D., age 20, has been in the United States Army since the age of 16, when he enlisted under a false name and false age. He is stationed at Panama, and will be discharged in March, 1928.

Pasquale's parents are Italian. The father came to the United States in 1904, and the mother in 1906. Five children were born, of whom 4 are living.

The father was a laborer, and provided for his family, but saved no money. When he died in 1918, of lobar pneumonia, his family was left destitute.

The mother was frail, and could do no hard work. Following her husband's death, she secured employment in the grocery shop of a brother-in-law. Some time later she went to live with him, as he was a widower. He was well off, owning a wholesale grocery business, and had his own home.

Three children were born to them, out of wedlock, in 1920, 1924 and 1925. The last child died. In 1925, Mrs. D. received nursing care from a welfare agency and was found to be an active case of tuberculosis.

Her own family at this time was scattered. One child was in a orphanage; one lived with an uncle in the Bronx; one was in the Army; and one child had died.

Rose, born in 1911, remained with her mother and the stepfather. In 1925, the mother died and her sisters sought in the Children's Court to secure the custody of Rose, pointing out that the step-father was not a moral man as he married Rose's mother only on her death-bed. It was insinuated that he intended to keep Rose as his mistress. The girl stated she was fond of her stepfather, but was satisfied to obey her aunt, and so made a home with her.

Pasquale was the oldest child. His developmental history is not known. A welfare agency quotes the mother as saying he was a misbehaved child who ran about on the streets and refused to attend school. Because of his troublesomeness, he was sent to the orphanage.

His school record covers the period from grade 3A to 5B. His work and conduct were average, but his attendance in the third grade was very poor. In 3A, he was absent 44 days. He was committed to the Truant school March, 1920, and remained until December. In April, 1921 he was again committed and remained nearly a year, until March, 1922.

His school behavior was described as lazy and indifferent. He smoked and spent his leisure time in the park and on the street.

When discharged from Truant school, he went to live with an uncle, as his mother was living out of wedlock and did not wish to be bothered with him. He remained there one year, working irregularly at 2 different jobs.

At the age of 16, he enlisted in the Army, where he has been for 4 years. He corresponds with his sister. His letters alarm her. As the time for his Army discharge approaches, his underlying instability shows itself. He writes of a different life plan in each letter, constantly changing his mind. He lives in phantasy, and tells her he has met a girl whose father is in business in California, and with whom he will obtain employment, after which he will marry the girl.

Case No. 3—Marco N., lives at home, works irregularly at a variety of unskilled occupations, and has had no police record since his release from Truant school.

The members of the family are unknown to social service agencies or to the police.

The father was born in Italy, in 1867, and came to the United States in 1890. He is over 60, yet works as a laborer for a power company, shovelling snow in winter.

The mother has been dead for many years. Since the boy's Truant school record was compiled, in 1921, the father has married his housekeeper.

The family has lived in two small rooms in Harlem, very near the East River, ever since Marco entered public school in 1912, and perhaps before that. The rent is $20. The rooms are light, airy, and fairly well-furnished. A great many pictures and knick-knacks are on the walls and tables.

Marco is the only child. His developmental history is not known. When interviewed, he stated he did not like school, and played on the streets during school hours with two like-minded pals. He laughed when he remembered the good times he had. His school record states that he was excitable and nervous. His behavior, work and attendance were average until grade 3B. In that term he was absent 48 days, and as a result found himself in the Truant school. Here he remained from May to October, 1921. Upon his return to day school his record was exemplary until he left, at age 16.

His present status was learned through a visit made to the home by a field visitor for the Sub-Commission on Causes.

He was interviewed regarding his past employment. He stated he was idle for a year after leaving school. Then he worked as a roofer's helper and later as a plumber's helper, earning $18 a week. During the past 3 months, he claims to be earning $30 a week, delivering grapes for a friend who has a market stall. This work, however, is only temporary and the season for it was just about over. However, the boy tried to give the impression it was permanent work. When the visitor offered to help him find a steady job, he said, "Thanks, I don't care to change."

He spoke of getting a chauffeur's license, but is so sluggish and dull that the visitor doubts his ability to qualify as a motorist.

He names his recreations as movies and dancing, and spoke disparagingly of marriage as requiring too much work of one, and only a means of wasting money.

He does not attend church.

Discussion: In Marco's case, commitment to the Truant school served to make a docile pupil out of him. But the same docility that served him in school, did not help him later. For a whole year after leaving school, he was idle. Somehow, the picture of Marco, docilely sitting in school until his sixteenth birthday, does not satisfy.

An educational program that drops a pupil with a thud when he leaves it, even though he is a dullard, requires change.

Case No. 4—In this case, the family is not known to social service agencies, nor to the police, and the boy's own statement must be depended upon. There is no police record, however, to contradict any of his statements and certain of them are corroborated by a Children's Court report on a younger brother.

Louis D. is now 21. He is unemployed at present, but claims to be earning a good salary in the building trades, as a laborer, and intends to marry soon.

The parents were born in Italy and came to the United States in 1898. They raised five children, all born in the United States, Louis being the third born.

The only record on the family is dated 1920, and is taken from the Children's Court.

The father, born 1872, was a porter, earning $20 a week. He was in good health. The mother, born in 1877, took care of her household.

In 1920, the family moved to Peru, Indiana, where they remained 2 years. Before moving, they occupied 4 well furnished rooms in a tenement house, paying $21 rental.

Nothing is known of the two oldest children.

Otto, born in 1908, was very backward in school, being in grade 2A at age 11. It was difficult to make him attend and he was on occasion carried to school kicking and screaming, by truant officers. A mental examination at the age of 11 years, 8 mo., disclosed he had a mental age of but 7 years, 2 months and an Intelligence Quotient of 61, placing him definitely among the feeble-minded.

Louis attended parochial school until grade 6A, when he transferred to public school. His conduct and work during 5 terms grew steadily worse, dropping from A to D. Likewise his illegal absence increased. He was committed to Truant school in April, 1920, and remained until October, 1920. His school conduct was described as "disorderly."

A field worker for the Sub-Committee on Causes, visiting the old home, chanced to meet Louis there. Her record of the conversation and her impressions are as follows:

"The former home of the D's. is in a particularly crowded section, where the streets are lined by markets. The population is largely Italian. The tenements are of the worst type; halls are dirty, without proper lights and means of sanitation. Toilets are in the hall.

This building is of brick, housing 16 families, with flats of 3 and 4 rooms.

The D's. moved about 5 years ago. However, they visit the old neighbors occasionally. Through suggestion of janitor V. called on an aged couple with a son of 22 years, whom I found at home, there finding Louis having lunch with them. Being unemployed he had come to see his old friend and schoolmate.

Louis is six feet tall, well built with rather classical Latin features, was somewhat reluctant to talk about himself, but shortly became friendly and told of early life. He was born and reared in this neighborhood, always enjoying good health, was interested in his school work until he reached the upper grades. He had many friends, was fond of athletics.

His pal, a boy by the name of R., always had a lot of money and supplied him with all that he wanted. They went to the movies, bought the best of things to eat rather than go home for meals. He soon lost interest in his studies. (The R. boy was in a lower grade.) They became truants, spent most of their time playing about and attending everything that went on at Madison Square Garden, whether they had the price of admission or not. Frequently they would sneak in and stay for days to see the bicycle races.

He said he had no difficulty with his teachers, nor were his studies too hard, but gave the teachers a great deal of trouble leaving the room without permission, disrupting the class. On these occasions he would run to find his gang. He just wanted a good time. His parents tried to discipline him and when he thought they were a bit too harsh he absented himself for days. Finally the parents decided that the best thing to do with him was to lock him up. They proceeded to chain him to a bed, but he got away and stayed for days. He was then admitted to a truant school but escaped and settled in a small Indiana town with friends. Later his father and brother went there and soon the whole family moved. After an absence of two years, they returned to New York and are living in the Bronx. He has been employed as a truck driver for a fruit concern, but in the past two years has been a helper in building trades, earning $9 per day and sometimes $65 per week. He is now unemployed and wants an up-to-date job. He feels that since he has a good knowledge of English and is American born he should command a good job although he is not skilled.

He describes his home as being comfortable. He states that his father and two brothers are working.

Louis has a girl whom he expects to marry. She is employed with a big insurance concern and he thinks she has been a good influence over him. ' She is the best girl in the world.' They attend church and social functions together, and her family think well of him.''

Discussion: Poor methods of home discipline and companionship with a boy of resource, who could devise exciting adventures, were outstanding factors in this case. Louis was not a delinquent and in fact showed much more ingenuity in finding enjoyable pastimes than does the average delinquent. He "lost interest in his studies" because the glamour of the old "Garden" was more real, its heroes more thrilling, than those the history books and geographies described. Schools face a monumental task in adapting the curriculum to create interest in sophisticated boys who have lived on the streets in a metropolis. But nothing short of genuine interest will keep spirited boys such as Louis glued to their desks.

Case No. 5 — Dominick B., age 19, lives at home. He has no trade, has worked at casual occupations, is now unemployed, and is suffering from a venereal disease contracted at the age of 15 when a victim of sodomy. He has no police record.

The parents came from Italy when Dominick was 1½ years old, in 1910. They asked for financial aid in 1912, and had until 1925 been known to welfare agencies.

The father, a furniture polisher, worked occasionally in a piano factory; his foreman said he was lazy. He has been ill since 1918, with asthma, and in 1920, had given up his trade, and had opened a candy stand which brought an income of only $12 a week.

He was a steady wine-drinker, apparently a man of dull brain, and little sense of responsibility, being anxious to have his wife work outside of the home to maintain the family. He is not a citizen.

The mother has worked frequently in a factory. In 1920, she was a finisher on dresses, earning $26 a week. She did the housework when she came home and was always very tired. In 1922, she attempted suicide, but the meter, operated by twenty-five cent pieces, was low in gas, and she was revived.

The family has moved twice since coming to the United States, once across the street, and once several doors down the street. In 1919, they lived in three bare rooms on the top floor, paying $11 rental. The bedroom was dark and ventilation was poor. When visited in 1927, five children and the parents lived in two rooms facing the Second Avenue Elevated. The rooms were large, and there was a piano, but hardly any other furnishings. There were no beds, but a sofa and a davenport. The home was clean, as the mother is not working. In the days when she worked, the home was described as dirty, forlorn and unkempt.

The home life in the earlier years was badly disorganized. The younger children were placed in day nurseries, and the older ones allowed to run the streets.

The subsequent history of the children is not known, except that the older daughter has been a dressmaker, is not married, and lives at home. The other children are still in school.

Dominick, was born in 1908, according to the school record, and in 1906, according to the father. His developmental history is not known. He was a T. B. suspect in 1918, but on examination proved to be free of the disease. His teeth were in bad shape and he required a tonsilectomy. He has had several injuries. Twice his arm was broken, once when hit by an auto while playing ball, and once when a taxi passenger, in a collision. He has had other less serious mishaps. In 1924, he was removed to the City Hospital for treatment of stomach trouble. Here an unknown man committed sodomy on him. He contracted a venereal disease, and still claims to be weak from its ravages. His eyesight is poor, but is corrected by glasses.

His school record is average for conduct and work. Up to the time he was committed for truancy, he had failed in two terms only. Truancy began in the second grade.

He was said to steal and gamble and spend leisure time either with a gang or in the movies.

He has been in the Catholic Protectory twice, in 1920 and in 1922, for six month periods.

In 1920, his father brought him to the Children's Court, charging him with incorrigibility, on the ground that he had remained away from home several days at a time on a number of occasions. The boy's own account of the events leading up to the last run-away is taken from the Children's Court record:

"I went to the grocery store to buy bread and another boy went with me. He stole three eggs from the store and threw them at another boy, who went to my father and said I threw them. And my father said I was going to get a licking. So I stayed away for four nights. I slept in a hallway, and sold rags and junk that another boy and I found in cellars. And we bought eats with the money.''

Dominick's free time was not his own. He took charge of his father's candy stand from 6:30 p. m. until 10 p. m. His real pleasures came while he was truant, and his favorite play-place was the river front.

He never attended church, nor was he ever confirmed.

When interviewed in December, 1927, by the field visitor from the Sub-Commission on Causes, he stated that his occupation was that of restaurant waiter, but he was unemployed at present. He says he cannot do heavy work. After leaving school, he did varnishing in a piano factory until the company went bankrupt. Later he learned pressing in a tailor shop, and worked at casual jobs, such as shoveling snow, etc.

His recreations are limited because of his bad eyesight. He does not go to the movies for this reason.

He impressed the field visitor as being a dull and slovenly boy.

Case No. 6—Frank R., age 21, lives at home and works steadily as a truck driver for a chemical house. He is a quiet, withdrawn type of boy, having few friends and limited interests.

The father was born in England and came to the United States in 1900. He was a bricklayer and worked steadily until 1920, when he suffered a stroke of paralysis. A year later, he was removed to a hospital, a helpless invalid, where he died in 1922. He was an unresponsive, withdrawn man, who made few friends and hardly knew the neighbors among whom he had lived for 20 years.

The mother who is still living, is of English birth, and has been in the United States since 1905. She is apparently of dull intelligence, has been a slovenly house-keeper, and has co-operated poorly with social service agencies. She has been neglectful of the health of her children, and has resented school inquiries into their absences.

The family occupies a four room flat in a tenement house. The front room is well furnished with upholstered furniture and a good rug. They have lived in these rooms for 20 years. The neighborhood is very poor. The home block is one street from the Hudson River and the section has had an unsavory name for years because of the thieves and gangsters said to come out of it.

There were six children.

The oldest son is married, and his present status is not known. He has had no police record. As a boy, he was in good health until age 14, when he suffered from an ear infection, contracted while swimming in the dirty waters of the Hudson River. He left school as soon as he could obtain working papers, worked irregularly, and made small contributions to the family. Shortly after his work history began he disappeared from home, remaining away several months. This ushered in a period of wandering and he was heard of from different parts of the country. Persuaded by his mother, he joined the Navy and enjoyed the life for a while but deserted his ship on the West Coast. He beat his way home and confessed his desertion. His mother influenced him to give himself up and he was confined in the Portsmouth Naval Prison for a time. The mother blamed the boy's bad company and irregular habits on neighborhood influences.

The oldest daughter is married to a taxi chauffeur. A second daughter worked for a film manufacturing concern, earning $18 a week. The youngest daughter attends Textile high school and has been encouraged by her mother to complete the course. The youngest child, age 11, attends school. He is frequently absent, with his mother's consent. He is a very excitable child. Two years ago he had a severe head injury and has since suffered from violent frontal headaches. He has received no medical care, although his mother realizes his skull may have been fractured.

Frank, born in 1906, seemed to be a very good pupil during his earlier years in school, receiving A and occasionally B in proficiency and deportment. He was known as a quiet child. He was different from the others, the mother said. His truancy began when he was transferred from the primary to the grammar school, in grade 6B. He found it difficult to adjust himself to the unfamiliar surroundings or to make new friends, and absented himself frequently. He was committed for five months to the Truant school, and took the punishment very much to heart, becoming downcast and aggrieved.

In 1921 he left school and obtained employment as a telegraph messenger. After being laid off he was idle for nine months. At that time he gave his mother much to worry about because he had begun to associate with undesirable companions living in the neighborhood, whom he had met down at the slaughter house at the docks where he had been while truant. The church secured several jobs for him, which he gave up readily. He was employed as an errand boy by the Parish house, but played crap while working and was otherwise unreliable. He attended Continuation school, albeit unwillingly.

Somehow or other, he learned to drive an automobile, "picked it up" as his mother described it, and has had a driver's license for several years. He is a chauffeur for a chemical house. His present work is physically tiring. He often works late and when he comes home, he usually eats and goes to sleep. Occasionally, he attends a movie. He belongs to no clubs or settlement houses and has very few friends. His mother claims he no longer associates with his former undesirable school friends, who have become loafers. He contributes regularly to the household. He has no ambitions.

The mother, when interviewed by the field visitor for the Sub-Commission on Causes, requested that the boy not be seen, as he was still sensitive over the commitment to the Truant school and would be upset if questioned.

Discussion: The case history describes an unstable boy who finds great difficulty in adjusting to new situations and who maintains balance only by living a routine life in which flexibility is not necessary. This type of adjustment is precarious and sudden larger responsibilities involving social adjustments, such as arise in marriage, would probably result disastrously. He is a boy who should have had every possible stimulus to participation in normal group life but who was not differentiated from his school-mates because his teachers did not recognize the significance of his withdrawn type of personality.

Case No. 7—Natale De R. was born in the United States in 1907. He is now 21, is married, lives with his mother-in-law and works at a vegetable push-cart.

The parents came to the United States from Italy 23 years ago. There were ten children, five daughters and five sons. The parents were illiterate and in spite of disciplining the boys by means of severe beatings, they had very little control over them. The father, who worked as a laborer died in 1924 of tuberculosis.

At that time the family occupied four rooms for which they paid $18 a month. The building was in a congested neighborhood, in which street gangs flourished.

The oldest son has been known to the police since 1920. He has been arrested for various offenses—disorderly conduct, sleeping in the subway, stealing groceries, and burglary. He spent two years in prison for selling narcotics. Prior to this sentence he was the joint owner of a small candy store that served as the rendezvous for his narcotics gang. He is at present living at home with his mother and is employed at a push-cart, selling vegetables.

The second son was arrested in 1920 for possessing a revolver without a license, but was acquitted. He is employed as a truck driver for a produce house.

The three youngest girls are attending school. One daughter, 16, is confined in a hospital, suffering from tuberculosis.

The youngest boy, now 20, is under-sized, mentally dull and without genuine ambition. For the past eight years he has worked for a vegetable dealer. He has a desire to be a taxi chauffeur.

The oldest girl left school as soon as she could be legally employed. After reaching the sixth grade, she stayed at home, and engaged in needlework, earning a small salary. She is said to have been a quiet, lovable and obedient child, who never was away from home late at night. During the latter part of 1927 she was arrested on the charge of homicide, having given birth in a hall toilet to an illegitimate child, which she in her fright, had killed and thrown into the back yard. The father of the child has just married her, and both are working in a shoe factory. The mother's lack of observation and dullness may be gathered from the fact that she was not aware of her daughter's condition, although they were together every day.

Natale seemed normal at birth and started school at the usual age. He attended regularly when young, but later became truant and associated with a street gang. He came home late and like his brothers and sisters, had much his own way. When he was 13, an older brother and he would go up on the roof and prowl around over the different buildings, coming home at noon and night for meals. This ruse worked so well that the parents were unaware of their truancy until the Attendance officer visited. Whippings followed, but these had little effect. A short truancy commitment was followed by the old habits.

In 1924 he ran away from home and his whereabouts were not known for some time. When he returned, he was eligible for working papers, obtained a push cart job, selling fruit and vegetables and worked steadily. He then became involved with a girl and was compelled to marry her.

The family does not approve of his marriage and have not visited Natale, although he has been married three years and has a child. He still sells vegetables from behind a push-cart.

Discussion: Unusual parental ignorance and street gang influences are outstanding points in this history. The roof stands out as a gang playground. The project has often been urged, of turning roofs in congested areas into gardens and supervised play spaces. Any one who has climbed over the roofs of New York buildings realizes that here is a vast amount of as yet unexploited space.

Case No. 8—Abraham A. was born in New York City in 1907. He is now 20, lives at home with his widowed mother and is employed in a moving picture studio, earning $40 a week.

The parents came from Austria 25 years ago. All of the children, four boys and two girls, were born in New York City. The father was in business, having a lease on a building which he rented out for weddings and other affairs. This netted the family a very adequate income until 1918 when the father became stricken with pneumonia and died.

The family occupied four rooms and a foyer on the top floor of this building. All save the kitchen were used for sleeping purposes. Although living in this building exposed the children to contact with undesirable crowds at late hours, none of them have become problems.

The mother, a stout, slovenly woman, when left a widow with six children found herself unable to cope with the responsibilities thrust upon her. In an effort to continue the business she lost what little control she had over her children. She discovered she had no business ability, and sold the lease to her brothers, who in compensation granted her free rental. The mother is now an invalid.

The oldest daughter, who worked in a moving picture studio, married one of the executives. Her husband is generous, contributing $25 a week toward his mother-in-law's support. Two other girls are working, one as a milliner and the other in a beauty parlor. The three youngest children attend school.

Abraham was normal at birth and never had serious illnesses. He began school at 6 and made good progress. He was an obedient child at home and was fond of his parents. Soon after the death of his father, his truancy became marked. His mother was distracted by her responsibilities and he led an independent life until all hours of the night. Two commitments to the Truant School, for eight and five months, respectively, seemed to sober him, for since his release he has worked steadily, first on a delivery truck for a department store and later in his brother-in-law's movie studio. He quit the truck job because he disliked wearing a uniform. In 1923, he was twice fined for violating traffic laws.

He attends evening school, learning the motion picture operating trade. His salary goes to maintain the household. When not at school, he reads a great deal.

The family atmosphere seems to be a happy one. The mother is planning to move to more desirable quarters so her children may entertain their friends.

Discussion: In this instance, truancy was co-incident with the breakdown of parental control following the father's death. Beneficial influences—the example of industry set by his sisters and the assistance of an influential brother-in-law have since aided the boy in setting a goal for himself. Of equal significance is the fact that he made good school progress and has the capacity for continued education.

Case No. 9—Dominick B. was born in New York City in 1907. He is now 20, and married. He lives in Brooklyn, works as a truck driver, and has been in no difficulty since school days.

The parents were born in Italy. The seven children, five girls and two boys, were all American-born. The family became known to welfare agencies in 1917, when the children were referred by the public school as neglected. The father was unemployed through illness, and the family of eight lived in two exceptionally dirty rooms. The mother earned about $5 a week, plucking feathers, and was forced to neglect her children to bring in this pittance. The family apparently was not without spirit and showed pride in being able to hold out for a long while against terrific odds, without asking for help.

The physical standards of the parents were, however, low and they were unmoved by appeals of social workers to make the home cleaner and more attractive. They used soap boxes instead of furniture. They refused to allow the children to have medical attention. They were unsociable and refused to allow the children's friends to enter the house. The welfare agency gave emergency help and closed the case.

In 1920, the school again referred the family for relief. They were found living in three filthy rooms. The oldest son, 19, has been under police observation for the past ten years. At 14, he was a juvenile delinquent, having committed a petty theft. At 17, he was convicted of burglary and sent to Elmira Reformatory. At 19, he was accused of robbery, but discharged. Two months later, he was sent to the workhouse for having possession of a revolver. He is known to associate with a crowd of bootleggers and thieves and is at present wanted by the police for participating in the "stick-up" of a club last month.

The other children have been well-behaved. Two are married, one girl works and three children are at school.

Dominick progressed steadily during his four first years at school, earning average marks. In the fourth grade, he got into difficulties with a teacher, conceived a great dislike for her, and became a confirmed truant, to such an extent that he had to repeat the grade six times. At the age of 12, he was sent to the Truant School, for six months and then recommitted, remaining until his 14th year. Upon his release, he secured employment and has kept out of bad company.

In 1927 he married a young telegraph operator. He is employed as a truck driver and lifts heavy cases. He is quoted by his mother as being sorry he left school because the work he does is harder than work he might have obtained through having a better education.

Case No. 10—Ferdinand R., now 20, is a careless, irresponsible boy, a "cake-eater," married by impulse to a girl he hardly knew and with whom he does not live, idle now, and recently implicated, by his own statement, in bootlegging operations. He has no police record.

Ferdinand is the oldest of five children. The father was born 1884, and the mother in 1886, both in Italy. The father came to the United States in 1904, and the mother in 1906.

The father was a brass worker. The earliest known facts on him are those recorded by the Department of Public Welfare, in 1917. He was then earning $14 a week, and was not a citizen, and had a previous record of deserting his family. In March, 1921, he again deserted. His wife complained in the Family Court that he had deserted her for another woman. A warrant was issued but never served. The father has never returned to his family. He lives in Chicago and sends $50 a month regularly.

The mother is ill, suffering from tuberculosis. She sews on coats at home. She does not read or speak English, and is not a citizen. She has accepted the responsibilities thrown on her, has resisted the idea that she is unable to care for her children, and has refused to allow them to be committed to institutions, although the offer has been made. She has not accepted other people's plans with good grace. In one instance she refused to allow several of the children to have tonsil operations urged by physicians.

Since the husband's desertion, the family of six have lived in two rooms, one of which is dark. There is no bath, and the toilet is in the hall. The rooms are hopelessly crowded, but are kept fairly clean.

Carmela, the oldest girl, born 1908, is working irregularly; Jose, born 1912, and Lucia, born 1916, are in school. Francesca, born 1920, had rheumatic fever and has a cardiac condition.

Ferdinand's developmental history is not known. Physically, he has been weak, and with poor resistance to disease. In 1917 and 1918, he had influenza and pneumonia. In 1919, his adenoids and tonsils were removed. In 1921, at age 14, he weighed 98 lbs. His mental status is not known. He has not been clinically examined.

His school record has been unfavorable. He reached grade 6-A, retarded six terms, repeating grades 1-A, 3-A, 4-B, 5-A (twice) and 6-A. His conduct averaged B, and work B—. His attendance was poor.

Truancy began in the first grade, and except in a few terms, continued throughout school life. He was ill-behaved at home, kept bad company, and remained out late at night. In November, 1921, several months before he would have been discharged as over-age, he was sent to the New York Truant School, where he remained 2½ months, until he was 16.

The period intervening between his release from Truant School, in February, 1922, and the home visit in December, 1927, has not been covered in any reports to this Sub-Commission, except that in February, 1927, he is reported as having worked in a factory on Long Island, earning $18–25 a week.

The home was visited in December, 1927 by a field visitor for this Sub-Commission. Her report is given verbatim.

"Found Ferdinand at home. The house is kept clean. The mother has been operated on for tubercular glands and finds it difficult to do much talking. Found that the husband is still away but sends his $40 or $50 regularly. The younger child, Francesca, is in Bellevue for almost 18 months, crippled with chronic rheumatism and heart condition. The other two children, Carmela and Jose, are both out of work; Carmela, 19, is learning zig-zag operation, Jose, 17, worked in a hat factory.

"Ferdinand is undersized, thin, but quite fussy as to appearance, with bell bottom trousers and patent leather shoes.

" 'Well, I got out of the Continuation school awright, and I fixed it so Joseph wouldn't have to go. No! I'm not working now, but first when I left school I used to work for my uncle in Asbury Park, just a few days a week, bootlegging, and I made good money. It's spoiled me because why should I work so hard and only get $20 or $25; but I was caught once but my uncle paid for everything — somewhere at Whitestone, L. I.— and then I gave it up.'

"He was working with a battery house but it closed down a while ago and he is idle since August, 1927. He hasn't saved any money, for he clothes himself and only once in a while gives the mother any. He seemed very affable and in good humor, keeping the family laughing most of the time.

"He has no especial recreation or interests. He is irresponsible, short-tempered, and cannot work in a place where the boss tells him what to do. 'If you don't like it this way do it yourself,' I tell him, and 'I take my hat and I'm troo.'

"He doesn't go to church at all, except on Christmas and Easter.

"He met a young girl this summer, knew her for less than a month, and went down to City Hall and was married, but discovered she had lied to him. She was only 15 instead of 19, and he has seen nothing of her since the marriage. He showed me the certificate in order to discover whether the marriage was legal. He is going to get rid of her but doesn't know just how.

"He thinks he would like to play a drum and traps in a band, but has no money. He has also been offered the chance to buy a pool room opposite Centre St. police headquarters, but doesn't know where he could get the $80 rent to pay.

"He doesn't seem to have any conception of responsibility or cooperation, and seems perfectly willing to hang around sponging on the earnings of the other members of the family.

"The mother appears rather good-natured and friendly, and was all for having me stay to 'coffee and cake' with the family.

"After some talk with Fredinand, he confessed it was all up to him. He would not ask anyone for any help, but would get a job and save his money so he could do the things he liked. He also realized that his chance of getting a good job was limited due to his meager learning and that he had no trade in hand, but is still determined that his uncle's bootlegging spoiled him for work. He promised to go out and get a job."

(Ferdinand's friend, who was present during our conversation, mentioned the fact that even though one did not have a regular job, there was plenty of money to be made from bootlegging and the white stuff—dope—at which Ferdinand gave him a threatening glance.)

Discussion: Here, "easy money" from boot-legging, is a deterrent to honest work with less spectacular returns. Child marriage intrudes. The old familiars—poverty, broken homes, neglect, are to be noted. But what is to be done? The reader cannot escape the conclusion that the home life as described in this and similar cases cannot be lifted by its own boot-straps, and success turned out of raw material such as Ferdinand, under the conditions imposed by his family circumstances. Unless adequate extra-family care is given to these children, in the form of daily supervision of recreation, daily adjustment of conflicts with others and daily evaluation of plans for the future, they are bound to fall, as parents, to the level of their own progenitors.

Case No. 11—Gustave O. was born in New York City 22 years ago in 1906. Two years ago he was known to have married, but lived with his parents, while his wife lived with hers. He was working as a chauffeur.

The parents came from Poland, though they were born in Germany. The father, in 1925, was a longshoreman, working on the docks. The mother was addicted to drink and was very quarrelsome.

The six children, born in the United States were housed with **the parents in 3 crowded rooms.** Home conditions were not very pleasant. There was a general air of untidiness and idleness, and the family frequently stayed in bed all morning.

The oldest daughter at 19 was decidedly defective. Her I. Q. at 16 was only 65, and she was very troublesome in school. She had been put in the ungraded class and had repeated nearly every grade. In 1925, she deserted her home and was found stranded in Norfolk, Va., where she had gone to meet a sailor with whom she was already known to have lived, and married him for fear she was pregnant. She then left New York and went to Norfolk to live.

The family then moved to less crowded quarters.

A younger sister, 12, was in 1925 held as a material witness with 4 co-defendants in a case of assault by a Greek shop-keeper. She was anaemic, had poor eyesight, decayed teeth and hypertrophied tonsils. According to her examination she was rated as a middle-grade moron, and it was urged she be committed to an institution for the feeble-minded. There was no special ability to warrant any training, and no marked emotional disturbance. Her sex delinquencies were marked, having been extended over a long period of time. Her companions were most undesirable, and upon investigation it was found that her sex relations had been quite promiscuous. In spite of all this, the mother refused to sign a petition for committing her to an institution for the feeble-minded. She was nevertheless remanded to an institution for delinquents in 1926.

Gustave himself progressed steadily in school up to the fourth year. His conduct was A and his work average B. But in the fourth year his contact with the gang, where he learned to smoke and gamble, soon affected his school work. His conduct was uncontrollable, his manner surly, and his absences very marked. The neighbors described him as "wild," and said that he took after his mother. At 15, in 1921, he was committed to the Protectory for 4 months. On his release he went back to the Opportunity class in the school, but within another 5 months was back in the Truant School and kept there 7 months until he reached his 16th birthday.

He was very irregular in his employment, and would often stay in bed all morning. He impressed one as being mentally defective.

At 19 he married, but due to his inability to provide means for a home and the responsibilities of supporting a wife, he was living with his parents, while his wife lived at her own home.

There is no data as to his employment, training, or present condition.

Discussion: In this case, as in several others, we glimpse in the children a continuation of the family cycle of ignorance, poverty and irresponsibility.

Case No. 12—Max R. was born in New York City in 1906 and is now 22. He is living with his widowed mother and is helping to support the family. He is working steadily as a driver on a milk wagon.

The parents came from Russia in 1896. Their twelve children coming at very short intervals were born in New York City. With the help of the older children the family seemed able to manage.

The father was a cloak finisher and worked irregularly. In 1918 he was run down and killed by an automobile, and it was then that several charitable agencies were appealed to for relief. Nothing of special interest is known of the father.

The mother, as a result of much child bearing and worry over finances, became sick and neurotic. She showed no stability and found it difficult to control the children even when they were very young, for they were abusive and struck her on numerous occasions. Several attempts were made to have her apply for her citizenship papers, but she refused to exert herself.

In 1918, two of the children were already married and were living away from home. The family was then living in 4 rooms and were supplied with rent, food and clothing by the charities.

The mother was most unco-operative, for she refused to allow any vocational plans to be made for one of the younger girls.

In 1922, when she was incapable mentally and physically of caring for the children, it was found necessary to commit the 3 youngest ones to foster homes. The mother was a cardiac, in addition was suffering from a goiter, and was extremely nervous. In spite of all that, her home was always immaculately kept and the children well cared for physically. But she continually complained, interfered, and would not give the children a chance to adjust themselves in the foster homes. She persisted in the belief that the children were being starved and neglected, in spite of their gaining weight, and since no headway could be made it was decided to place them in an orphan asylum where she could interfere less.

In 1926 the family occupied a six room apartment in the East Bronx. The rooms are large, sunny and well ventilated.

The three eldest children are married, and have families of their own. Nothing of special importance is known of them, with the exception of one daughter who seemed to have more influence with the mother than any of the children. It was through her that any medical care could be given to the mother or the younger children.

According to the reports from the social agencies to whom the family has been known since 1915, there has always been a problem of delinquency among the older sons, for the three have police records. Two of them enlisted illegally in the army and marines. Deserting the service, they were jailed. One boy disappeared and his whereabouts were unknown. Another boy was beyond parental control and he was sent to the Jewish Protectory, from which he escaped and was later arrested as a vagrant in another state. No regular support of any kind was obtained from any one of them.

In 1921, a daughter, 18, was sent to a sanitarium, being suspected of tuberculosis.

Another daughter, 15, had applied for working papers in an effort to contribute to the support of the family.

A 14 year old girl has been difficult from time to time, both at home and at school, and is being treated at a pediatric clinic.

The 3 youngest, 2 girls and a boy, were examined psychologically at the orphan asylum. It was found that the girls were borderline defectives. The youngest boy was very nervous, stammered, ate very little, and was untidy in his habits. His work in school was very poor. At times he was most troublesome. He had a habit of sleeping in his clothes, and yet seemed very willing to be of help at all times.

Max, being one of 12, did not get very much individual attention. His school work was poor, so was his attendance. His truancy manifested itself in the kindergarten, for he repeated that class three times. His progress was slow, and in 3A and 4B he was again retarded twice.

In 1921, at 15, he was committed to an orphan aslyum, but ran away a number of times and was finally sent home. At that time a mental test showed him to be only 12 years and 3 months mentally, placing him in the dull group. He was also found to have an enlarged cervical gland. His mother said that he was unruly, and he refused to attend school. He also quarreled with the other children and struck the mother. Just at that time he left home for 6 months, so he would not have to attend school and the mother had no knowledge of his whereabouts.

In January, 1922 at the age of 16, he was sent to the Truant School and discharged after 8 months.

After this experience the boy seemed to improve and to take an interest in the home. He worked unlawfully, without working papers for about 6 months.

In 1923, at 17, he was operated on for hernia, and after that became more steady in his habits. He worked as a shipping clerk and was anxious to attend a vocational school at night so he could learn automobile mechanics.

According to the last report, Max is much devoted to his mother and sisters. The mother claims he is a source of comfort to her. He is earning $35 a week steadily as a driver on a milk wagon.

Discussion: In this case, some unknown causes changed Max from a troublesome runaway into a steady worker. The only apparent cause is the hernia operation. It is, of course, possible that relief from the chronic irritation of hernia might have been a major factor in his change.

The emphasis on social and mental factors often obscures the importance of physical conditions that underlie behavior considered erratic.

Case No. 13—Tony R. was born in New York City, February, 1906, of Italian parents. The father, Pietro, had come from Italy in 1898. He was a painter.

The family first came to public notice in 1920. In that year, Tony was arrested for forcing his way into a grocery store on the home block, and in company of a friend and an older half-brother, stealing $15 of foodstuff. Tony had been a model boy, with excellent school attendance and conduct until Grade 5B, when truancy and bad behavior set in. In Grade 6A, 100 days of illegal absence

and conduct rating of D were recorded. He spent his spare time on the streets. The principal attributed his delinquencies to bad companionship. The boy's statement upon arrest reveals gross lack of home control:
"I went to the movies with my half-brother at 3 P. M. and remained until 11 P. M., the end of the performance. At 11:30 we met my friend, and my half-brother said he was going to 'make a hit' some place. We watched out for cops and he broke open the window and went in the store. When we saw a cop we ran up on the roof and slept until 5 A. M., then we stole two bottles of milk, and went to a bakery to steal bread, but were arrested. We stole in a butcher store, getting $11.50. I got $2.50 as my share. We steal apples and other fruit and sell them and buy cigarettes. I smoke eight a day."

Tony's mother was dead and the father had remarried, to a widow with children. The father earned $18 a week, and nine lived in four rooms, paying $14 rent. The stepmother was janitress.

Two months later, while on probation for the above offense, he was committed to the New York Truant School, and transferred to the New York Catholic Protectory.

In 1924, the father suffered a paralytic stroke and the resulting hemiplegia disabled his right arm, incapacitating him for his regular employment. The hospital referred him to an employment bureau for handicapped men, but he never accepted any of the jobs offered and did not appear anxious to work, although he repeatedly asked for jobs. He could not read or write English and spoke poorly, despite 27 years in the country.

In September, 1924, Nicolo, born in 1914, was arraigned in the Children's Court for stealing, in company with a friend, a package from an auto. Probation followed. In April, 1925, Nicolo stole, also in company, shoes from a store. He named the corner grocer and neighbors in his tenement building as receivers of property he previously stole. Nicolo was a mental defective, I. Q. 61, easily influenced by others. The judge committed him to Letchworth Village, an institution for mental defectives.

Family conditions were worse in 1925. The father earned $10 a week on the average. A new daughter was born, and eight children were sleeping in 3 beds. The children were neglected, a girl of 7 suffering with a skin disease. The family case work agency which had begun giving relief in 1924, reported as follows on the family: Stepmother has syphilis, tertiary stage. Oldest daughter is married. Mother's oldest son in N. Y. City Reformatory on felony charge. Mother's daughter, errand girl, is feebleminded. Younger school children retarded, infants at home dirty and neglected. Home in filth and disorder.

Tony in 1924, was small, timid, halting in speech, despite his 19 years. At home, however, he was insolent and non-cooperative. He contributed only $2 a week and insulted his father when asked for more. His work record during the period, 1924–26 was:

1924—worked in laundry managed by friend of mother, $15 a week.
1925—driver.
1926—delivery boy, earning $35–45 a week.

In 1926, as soon as his wages increased, Tony married. His civil marriage took place at City Hall.

In 1927, the field visitor for this Sub-Commission visited the home of the parents, and found it dirty, cold, and the children ragged. The stepmother had quarreled with Tony's wife and no longer spoke to her. The girl is American, non-Italian.

Tony, when visited at his home, was minding his infant with every sign of paternal fondness. His wife appeared to be more refined than he, and better educated. Tony drives a laundry wagon.

Discussion: Tony was superior to his family background, which was checkered by mental deficiency in both father's and stepmother's heredity, and by syphilis. Congested quarters, dirt, parental neglect, produced two truants and a thief. The latter had a bad influence on Tony, who improved when the other was sent to prison. The fortunate marriage and apparent adjustment promise well for the future.

Case No. 14—Terence W. was born in New York City in 1908. He is now 20, and lives at home. He works irregularly, and occasionally gives his pay to the mother.

The father, born in Ireland, came to this country 30 years ago and is at present working in the capacity of stable foreman.

The mother, also born in Ireland, has been in this country 32 years.

The family, consisting of five boys and a girl, were all born in the United States. The income has been sufficient for them to manage, since they are unknown to any charitable organization. They seem to be steady people, not desirous of many changes for bettering themselves, for they have been living in the same rooms for 20 years, and have a very good reputation in the neighborhood.

There are no outstanding police records against the family, two of the older brothers have been arrested, one for reckless driving, and the other for being intoxicated.

Terence seems to be the one who has given most trouble. The others are working steadily and contributing towards the upkeep of the house.

Terence was very disobedient and was uncontrollable to such an extent that in 1924, at 16, his mother committed him for three months to the Catholic Protectory. In spite of repeating the two last years in school, he managed to graduate at a little over 13 years, according to the statistics concerning his birth record. His truancy was most apparent in the seventh and eighth grades of school, and he was sent twice for a term of five months each to the Truant School when he was 12 and 13. Since his release from the Protectory he has been arraigned four times for violation of his parole, and until 1924 was under the supervision of the Court

When interviewed in 1928, the mother stated that Terence is out late nights and associates with "bold girls," and she does not approve of his companions. He was persuaded to join the "Y" last year, but did not renew the application this year. He has always been clothed by his parents in spite of his unsteady work. His family has no knowledge of his present work or employer. He seems the black sheep in the family.

Discussion: In this case, a mother of apparently more than average energy has applied severe treatment to a boy who in many other more negligent families would have been allowed his own way.

Terence is not a criminal, nor even a misdemeanant. Had sufficient attention been paid to the causes of his misbehavior at the age of 12, when he was committed for truancy, his habits might have been re-directed to insure regular living.

Case No. 15—Pietro N's. parents started house keeping with three rooms in the rear of a six story tenement, paying $16.00. Pietro, the youngest of four children, was born December 12, 1909.

In 1919 when Pietro was ten years old, the father died of a stroke. Now the burden fell on the mother's shoulders. The two girls helped shoulder the load by working and contributing their share so the family could be kept together. But Pietro was a problem. His mother seemed unable to get him to obey her and fearing that the future might bring more trouble, she applied to the Department of Public Charities in an effort to have him committed to an institution. That year seemed a hard one for Pietro too. Just at this time his teacher in school became provoked at Pietro's conduct and unfortunately lost control of her temper and slapped him. This treatment from his teacher aroused such resentment in Pietro that though he had progressed steadily up to the fourth year his animosity got the better of him and he refused to go to school.

Nothing could be done with him so he was sent to Truant School in December, 1919, and kept there until March, 1920. Upon his release he went back to school and somehow in spite of his mother's plea Pietro found himself again with the teacher who had struck him. The situation became tense and Pietro found that the streets were more to his liking than the school room. And in August he was caught entering a place where he broke a number of articles, but he was put on probation. His non-attendance brought him another term in the Truant School and he was kept there from August, 1920 to March, 1921.

His mother had her hands full now because his older brother at 15 (in 1920) was arrested for stealing two packages from a wagon, but was put on probation. Then in June, 1921 at 16, the brother failed to attend school and a fine of $2.00 had to be paid.

In 1923, when Pietro was 14, he was again brought to court on a charge of indecent behavior. He was accused of improper conduct toward two girls who were in his school class and was given a suspended sentence. He claimed that he had no wrong intentions and that the girls flirted with him. They had written notes to him asking that he take them to the movies, but that he had no money to do so.

That seemed the last in the way of trouble for Pietro for after reaching the 6-B grade he left school. In an effort to support himself he shined shoes, carried luggage and sold papers. In 1925 his mother died and his older sister, who was now married, made a home for Pietro. His brother-in-law is a butcher and has employed Pietro steadily, first as errand boy, and now he is teaching him the trade. Pietro is earning $20.00 a week and is happy. He has no bad habits, smokes a little, but does not drink. He spends his leisure hours at a social club or a movie, or sometimes at home listening to the radio. He is extremely fond of his sister's children and devotes much time to the one who is named after him.

Discussion: Pietro was an energetic, fun-loving boy who ran afoul of school discipline and a teacher who was free with her hands. None of his offenses were a result of viciousness, but of destructiveness and of sex curiosity. One must question the wisdom of the school principal who was willing to rub salt on a raw wound by arranging Pietro's return to the class-room teacher who was responsible for his Truant school commitment. This may have been good "discipline," but poor common sense and poorer mental hygiene.

Case No. 16—Anthony M. is 21 years old. He was forced to marry a sixteen year old girl and is now working hard as a truck driver to support his wife and child. Prior to marriage, he loafed.

The father, born in Italy in 1878, came to the United States in 1882, and in 1920, he had his first papers. He was a glass beveler, his earnings averaging $40 a week. In 1925, he was arrested and placed on probation on a felonious assault charge. He died in 1926.

The mother, born in 1886, takes care of her household. In 1922, she was arrested for illegally possessing a .38 calibre revolver, but was discharged.

The family is English-speaking, and according to the principal of the private school attended by the children, is less docile than most immigrant families. Health agencies and teachers complain of the unusual secretiveness and non-cooperativeness of this family. Important health work had to be neglected because the members would not consent to treatment.

The children were recently examined by the school physician and found to be under great nervous tension. The family is suspected of selling and using narcotics.

They have lived for over 15 years in the same four rooms, in a congested downtown district. The sanitary conditions have varied, being described at times as clean and other times as dirty. The children slept three in a bed. At present, five children are still at home.

May, the oldest girl, worked in a paper box factory. Peter, born 1909, is 16. He lives at home, works as a clerk, and attends evening high school, in preparation for law.

The younger children, who are in school, have negative histories
Anthony, born January, 1907, in New York City, is the second child and the oldest boy. His developmental history is not known. His teeth were poor, and he had dental clinic care in 1922 and 1926. His vision is corrected by glasses. At 15, he smoked cigarettes. He is now thin and pale, but claims good health.

His school record shows average conduct and inferior scholastic standing. He was not a serious truant until the 7-A grade. He completed the 8-A grade.

His commitment to Truant school apparently followed a serious misunderstanding between him and his teacher. The latter, a man, struck him for some infraction of rules, and Anthony, in anger, refused to attend further sessions. He was described at this time by his teacher as being defiant, disobedient, and lazy. This description is in marked contrast to his A conduct marks in the upper terms, and must be regarded as biased.

He appears to have been influenced by a street gang. Ten days before his commitment to Truant school, he was arraigned in the Children's Court on a charge of having, in company with other boys, thrown bricks from a roof. He offered the alibi that he had been in the movies with a friend, and the charge was dismissed.

He remained in Truant school from May to December, 1920. In April, 1921 he was re-committed. In June, 1921 he escaped. (When interviewed in 1927, he displayed pride in this achievement and stated he had gotten into difficulty at Truant school for refusing to join the band.)

His conduct subsequent to his escape was markedly worse. He never returned to school, and worked in a wet wash laundry. In 1922, he was arraigned again in the Children's Court, on the charge of robbing a Chinese laundryman of $15. The investigation disclosed that he associated with a gang that stole from fruit stands, came home late evenings, attended movies four evenings a week, smoked, and neglected his church duties. The arresting officer testified that Anthony had a bad reputation in the home neighborhood, and stated the boy had held up another man who had refused to press charges.

The wet wash laundry, where he had worked illegally, described his services as satisfactory.

Anthony's alibi was that at the time the alleged robbery took place, he was in the movies with a friend. This alibi was successful two years before, but failed now. He was placed on probation and ordered to complete his Truant school commitment.

His work record, subsequent to his release from Truant school, is:

April—Sept., 1922—truck helper—$14 week.

Sept. 5, 1922—glass beveler—$12 week; secured job through father. Worked three weeks and quit as work was heavy and firm objected to Continuation school.

Sept. 25, 1922—job in wet-wash laundry, $3 day, three days a week.

Oct. 1922—truck helper with old employer—$14 week.
During this time he gave his earnings to his parents and received an allowance which he spent.

There is no record of his progress during the next four years. In September, 1924 he was arraigned for participating in a crap game. The case was dismissed. When interviewed in 1927, he stated he has worked as a truck driver at $30 a week during the past six months only. Before that he was idle and was in debt. He gave the impression of disliking work.

He is now living with his wife, a 16-year old Italian girl, whom he married in the spring of 1927. His wife attended high school, taking a stenographic course. Their baby, a sickly child, is now nine months old, and the girl-mother plans to secure work when when the baby is older. She claims to have been a stenographer in a law office.

Their home life is uneventful. Anthony spends most of his evenings in the house as his work is tiring. On holidays they sometimes take in a show. He and his wife are on friendly terms with his family.

Discussion: The concept of the school as a place for teaching children how best to live precludes corporal punishment. But in spite of concepts to the contrary, and of emphatic board rulings human nature in this instance asserted itself.

This, from the point of view of sound education, is deplorable. A process of child training that develops grudges, as it did in the case of Anthony M., and that puts a premium on might, rather than on right, comes dangerously close to original human nature itself.

What machinery exists in the school system to-day whereby an outraged and muscular adult and a recalcitrant but defenseless pupil can meet on a plane of equality in the consideration of the respective merits of their cases?

It seems that this is a juncture at which the term "democracy" might well take living form.

Case No. 17—Mario R., 21 years old, born in New York City in 1907, has lived away from home two years, having quarreled with his parents. He is living with an American-born girl, states he is married to her, and claims he works steadily as a baker.

The parents came from Southeastern Italy in 1900, and reared a family of nine, all born here, whom they were unable properly to support. They have been in want, and on a number of occasions have appealed for charitable aid. In 1919, assistance was refused, and the family was labelled "un-cooperative."

In 1913, the father was a hod carrier, earning $2.50 to $3.00 a day, working steadily. Subsequent records indicate he was a regular worker. Nothing adverse is known regarding his character or traits. He had no police record.

The mother, in addition to rearing nine children, was janitress of the tenement house in which they lived. She was too busy to care for her home, and in the days when the children were young, the rooms were dirty. She has retained her old-world-traits, for example, has never learned English.

The family has lived for more than 15 years in the same block. The original residence consisted of two three-room scantily furnished ground floor apartments, granted rent free in consideration for janitor services.

A visit in 1927 disclosed that five children are still at home. The family live in a less desirable apartment than formerly, occupying only three rooms, facing the Second Avenue Elevated. It was poorly furnished, but clean.

The oldest child, a boy, and the oldest girl were suspected in 1913 of having tuberculosis and given preventorium treatment. The girl died in 1918 of pneumonia. The oldest boy worked as a driver. He is now living away from home, presumably married.

Mario's developmental history is not known. His school record was better than that of most of the children in this study. Up to Grade 6B, his attendance was regular and he had been regularly promoted. In this grade he began to be truant, and failed of promotion twice. He reached the 8A grade. His marks in work were usually B and sometimes B plus. His conduct was A and B. His only bad habit was gambling for money stakes.

He was committed to the Truant school at age 12, having been absent 45 days from school. He remained from December, 1919, to May, 1920. A year later he was re-committed for two months.

His only Children's Court record occurred in 1921, and on this occasion he appears to have been the victim of an older boy's plan. With two friends and a boy of 17, they took a horse and wagon for what Mario thought was a joy-ride. The older boy tried to sell the outfit and all were arrested. Mario was placed on probation.

His mother, when interviewed in December, 1927, by a field visitor for this Sub-Commission, stated that Mario had associated with bad companions when a boy. She characterized him as now being nervous and temperamental. She concealed the fact that he was living away from home, and only through a neighbor was it learned that he left following a quarrel.

Mario himself, met by chance in front of the baker shop where he worked, stated he married an American girl two years ago. Both of them work, the girl being employed in a radio factory. They live in a three-room apartment. They have no children and are anxious not to have any.

He stated he has been employed in bakeries since leaving school, and steadily employed since his marriage. He earns $32 a week. His hours are long—at present he works nights, 10 p. m. to 8 a. m. —and he is eager to have a job that is less "tough," as he puts it.

Discussion: If the summary on this case is scanty, it is because the available data on this boy's history are decidedly inadequate. The records of the schools are eloquently silent regarding the causes for Mario's truancy after six years of good scholarship. There is a strong suggestion of influence by older and more daring boys, taking place during a period of adolescent instability. The mother's characterization of him suggests that the instability still continues.

Yet Mario was not given the kind, studious attention that adolescents merit. There was no one to question why at 11 he was a good pupil, and why at 12 he was absent 45 days out of the term. It is cases such as this that often present gratifying recoveries when the difficulty, often simple, is laid bare through clinical study.

Case No. 18—Victor P., age 21, lives at home. He earns very little, working at rough labor. At present, he works three to five days a week, unloading bananas at the docks. He is saving money for good clothes, so he may meet a girl who will marry him.

The father, age 54, was born in Italy and came to the United States in 1903. He is a laborer, works irregularly, and has had an average income of $12 a week. In 1925, he was injured, and in a city hospital. He is not a citizen, and is illiterate.

The mother, age 50, was born in Italy and came to the United States in 1904. She is in good health, is illiterate, and on occasion has supplemented the family income by night work as a scrubwoman.

The family income averages $45 a week and has never been enough, the family consisting of two adults and nine children. A family welfare agency has given aid over a period of 13 years.

The home neighborhood is poor and congested. The family of 11 persons have lived since 1907 in four poor rooms, paying $20 rent. The home atmosphere has been congenial, but moral standards have been low, due to ignorance. There is no police or Children's Court record on any member of the family.

The oldest girl, born in 1904, is married.

The next in order, born 1908, died in 1926 of septic meningitis.

A daughter born in 1912 works in a candy factory at $9 a week.

The two youngest daughters are still in school. One, age 13, is in 8A; one, age 11, in 4B, suffers from rheumatism.

A boy of 19 works irregularly as a truck driver, earning $4 a day when he works.

Victor, born in November, 1906, is the oldest boy, and the oldest child now at home. His developmental history was normal; he was a large, well baby. At the age of 10 he had pneumonia.

There is no record of a mental examination, but he is obviously mentally defective, and has been in ungraded classes in school.

His school record shows irregular attendance, fair conduct, and average work until the fifth grade, when he seems to have reached the limit of his capacity. Subsequent marks were C and D. He was in ungraded classes until 4A.

He is described as having been very mean and sneaky, smoked and gambled. His leisure time was spent on the street.

In May, 1920, at the age of 14, he was committed to Truant school for 7 months. He returned, and remained in school until the age of 17, leaving in 1923.

His occupations have been of the simplest type. When a schoolboy he blacked boots. Since, he has driven a horse and wagon, irregularly, for one employer, earning $10 a week. He contributes $6 of this to his family. They consider him extravagant because he spends part of his own portion on clothing. He belongs to no clubs, has not been in church since the age of 11. He has few boy friends, and goes to movies with girls not known to the family. He realizes he cannot marry on $10 a week, yet has the feeble hope of winning a girl if he can get hold of some good clothes. He has no delinquency record.

Discussion: This case is illustrative of the inconsistent effect upon conduct of both native factors and social environment. This family, handicapped by inadequate intelligence, illiteracy, poverty, and congestion has nevertheless reared law-abiding children. It is perhaps significant in this connection that the parents themselves have been law-abiding.

It is undoubtedly of importance that over a span of 13 years these people have had the advice and assistance of more intelligent members of the community, in the form of family welfare care. Probably of greatest importance, however, is that the home life has been unimpaired and congenial. Had it not been congenial, the children would undoubtedly have gone their separate ways and perhaps gotten into difficulties. Had the home been broken, parental control would have been less strong and there would have been less pressure on Victor to turn in the major part of his earnings.

Low mentality, as this case shows, is not necessarily a basis for crime. However, eugenists would be justified in pointing out that Victor's marriage would hardly be of benefit to posterity. Less biological-minded but more pragmatic persons would say that Victor's domestic future is bound to be precarious. So far, he has led a fairly sheltered existence. One can but conjecture what difficulties will ensue from the marriage of an irregularly employed dullard, who in these days of high wages and high prices can command only $10 a week, and whom school and institution have not aided in becoming sufficiently self-supporting to maintain the progeny he will undoubtedly beget.

Case No. 19—Samuel B., born in New York City in 1906, now 22, lives at home with his mother and two younger sisters. He works irregularly, as helper in a fruit store or at a vegetable stand, and at present has been idle for eight weeks.

The parents came from Warsaw, Poland, more than 20 years ago. They have been in want due to the father's illness and have appealed for aid to charitable organizations on several occasions.

In 1920, the father was working as a clothes presser earning $45 a week, although he was constantly ill. Upon thorough examination he was found to be in the second stage of pulmonary tuberculosis. After treatment and medical supervision it was necessary to send him to a home for incurables. Though the family was pleasant and co-operative at that time, there seemed to be very little parental control.

The mother was also ill and given hospital care for some internal condition for a short period.

They were living in four rooms on the lower East Side, in a most congested neighborhood, paying a rental of $20. There were five children in the family, three girls and two boys. The mother was unable to manage her family. Just as soon as the father was committed, a very unwholesome spirit prevailed, and the mother had to appeal for charitable aid.

The oldest daughter worked as forelady in a factory and married eleven years ago. She is the only loyal person in the family, for in spite of having a husband whose work is seasonal, she somehow manages to save a little now and then to help her mother, occasionally paying the rent. She seems very discouraged at the lack of spirit and interest in the younger brothers and sisters.

In 1920 the oldest boy, then 17, ran away and joined the Army. Since then, he has made no attempt to contribute anything towards the support of the mother. In fact, he never communicated with them, and they know nothing concerning him, except that he is at Langley Field in Virginia.

One of the younger sisters graduated from Junior High School and the mother decided that she had better go to work and help. If she was desirous of advancing, she could go to school at night. The girl was given vocational guidance, and though she was placed at different times, appeared very indifferent to work. She was shiftless and could not hold a job for any length of time. She is now 20, has no definite training (her mother claims she is very handy with the needle) working for very short periods with very long intervals of unemployment. Her earnings have never been over $14 a week, and she has no sense of cooperation for she makes no attempt towards supporting the household.

Both the mother and the older sister, when interviewed, felt that she was a problem and are most discouraged and concerned over her. Up to a year ago, she used to attend a social settlement and had many young friends, but now gives up her entire time to her "young man." The "young man" is middle-aged, his whereabouts are unknown, his profession that of a bootlegger. All attempts to have her drop him have been useless. The family are convinced he is a member of a gang, and fear his influence over the girl. They are also certain that he will never marry her; and there is keen antagonism shown by her towards the mother and other members of the family.

The youngest girl is still attending school.

There is no detailed information of Samuel's progress in school, but it is known he was dull and difficult to manage. At 15 he became a decided truant and was beyond his mother's control. Home conditions then were poor and poverty was prevalent. Though Samuel was encouraged to help the family, he was not cooperative and could not be induced to remain at any one job. He had to be urged to attend Continuation School.

In June, 1922, he was arrested for stealing electric bulbs, but was given a suspended sentence. Five days later he was sent to the Truant School for a month.

Through a vocational guidance bureau he was examined physically and mentally. He was found to be normal physically with the exception of markedly impaired vision.

In general abstract intelligence he rates as dull normal. He approximates the average boy of 15 in manual dexterity and manipulation, but had no ability to deal with abstracts, e.g., numbers, words, or symbols. This uneven development probably explained his apparent laziness and lack of interest in school work. Also, the fact that in his class he associated with boys younger and smaller than himself may also have accounted for his attitude. The mental clinic at that time advised that he be given training in a skilled trade, but Samuel could not be persuaded to undertake this. He was shiftless and could not hold any job that was secured for him. He preferred working in factories and at fruit stands.

A visit to the home in January, 1928, disclosed that 3 of the children are at home. It is 5 years since the social agencies have ceased supporting the household, and the mother is at a loss, for the 2 older children are not dependable, and she herself is not capable of much work. Occasionally she goes out cleaning, but her rheumatism bothers her and she has a hard time. The family is at present living in the Bronx, in 5 rooms at $50. The mother said that she moved because she thought it might help get rid of the daughter's " young man.'' Though they live in a congested neighborhood, the rooms are light and kept immaculately clean. A widow and 2 children share the rent and general expenses.

Samuel applied for a chauffeur's license, but due to his impaired eyesight was refused. He is very fussy about his " good looks '' and will not wear glasses. Up to a little while ago he used to attend clubs at a social settlement, but now spends most of his time with his friends. He strives to imitate them, but cannot afford it, as their fathers are all in businesses of their own and the sons work for them.

He has confessed that he wishes he had taken the opportunity of learning a trade, and has gone to the charities in an effort to get a job with regular hours so he can learn some trade at night, as the hours in the fruit and vegetable trade do not allow for any time to be spent in evening school. His mother feels that it is his own fault for losing his job, because he takes advantage of the boss' good-nature, taking a day off every now and then and dawdling on the job.

Nothing anti-social is known of his conduct, and he has given his mother no trouble since his release from Truant School.

Discussion: This case is an illustration of sheer economic waste. Samuel B. is good material. He is not a delinquent. His truancy began only when family life fell into confusion over the sudden removal of the father. He could not be persuaded to work at anything requiring precision or skilled movements. No one, not even the clinic that advised he learn a skilled trade, saw any relationship between his desire for rough labor, and his defective eyesight. Yet it appears obvious that without correction of this handicap, nothing else could be done for him.

Having never worn lenses, Samuel had never really learned precision, and therefore could not appreciate how much of life he was missing through dim eyesight. Yet there was no one to picture enticingly enough for him the pleasures of good sight, or to advise him in ways of achieving good looks, other than at the expense of vision. Had someone even been willing to provide him with a really *good-looking* spectacle frame, perhaps he might be a skilled mechanic to-day.

To some this may seem like an over-simplification of the problem. It is true that many steps would have been necessary to raise this boy's interest to the point of entering a trades career, yet all other efforts would have had to center on overcoming the initial handicap in vision. For such a boy more than a doctor's prescription was necessary. In the absence of intelligent, and imaginative guidance, he has been an almost total economic loss.

Case No. 20—Louis D. is 22 now, having been born in New York City in 1906. He is employed as a plater on silver work, and lives at home with his parents. His work at present is irregular as business is slow.

The parents came from Italy 27 years ago, bringing a little girl with them.

The father was a shoemaker and earned only $9 a week. Nothing anti-social is known of him.

The mother has apparently no outside contact, for after 20 years in this country she is as yet unable to understand English. With her ignorance of American customs it was very easy for the children to deceive her. They would take their books and go along with the other children, but did not go to school. Her ignorance made her unwilling to co-operate, even when it was a question of helping herself. In 1926, she was suffering with a leg ailment, but refused any medical treatment. In 1927, when the home was visited, the mother appeared antagonistic and unwilling to speak until it was explained to her that no harm was meant.

In 1917, they were living in three rooms, which were housing nine members in the family. Although the neighbors spoke well of the parents, it seemed a hard job to control the boys in such crowded quarters. The father tried his best to get the children to attend school, and at times was compelled to take them himself.

In 1926, the family was living in four rooms. The toilet out in the hall was used by two families.

There are 7 children.

The three older girls have married, and the family income has diminished, so that in 1927 the family was living in two rooms facing the Second Ave. Elevated. They were clean but poorly furnished. Up to the time of their departure from the home, the three older girls worked in a shirt factory earning $8 a week apiece.

In 1925, the youngest boy, who was then only 10, was arrested for trying to open women's handbags, but was given a suspended sentence. When last seen, he was playing the violin and seemed much interested in his playing.

Louis, born 1906, progressed steadily the first three terms in school. His work was marked B and B plus. But in the fourth grade he was demoted for three terms due to his lack of interest and truancy. His father was compelled to bring him to school, and when not watched he would run out. The teachers complained of his bad conduct, and were annoyed by his continual laughter.

In 1916, when he was 10, he was arrested for stealing a quantity of copper wire, and was placed on probation. The older boys with whom he was associating are thought to have influenced him. Also, at this time, while playing with the gang on the roof, he fell and hurt himself. His father attributed his later bad conduct to the result of the injuries resulting from that fall.

In 1917, Louis was sent to the Catholic Protectory for stealing oranges.

At that time his physical examination showed no neurological signs, nor symptoms of any serious illness.

He was not found to be feeble-minded, but the mental test showed he was retarded 2 years. During that interview he was depressed and cried readily. He often said he was sorry for his past conduct. It was suggested that he be given individual training under some Big Brother, one preferably with pedagogic training.

His stay at the Protectory did not improve him, for in September, 1921, at 15 he was committed for truancy and kept at the Parental School for 8 months. Nothing is known of his development since his discharge in 1922.

In December, 1927, when interviewed, he frankly answered most of the questions, but would give no information concerning his work status.

He is well developed, in good health, and rather good looking. He appeared phlegmatic and slow. His display of temper was shown when he snapped at his younger brother for playing the violin. He was reading a tabloid newspaper, but nothing could be learned about his outside interests, either social or otherwise.

He said that business was slow, but it was no fault of his. He acknowledged his regret in not having attended school regularly, and promised that if ever he had children he would see to it that they did not become truants. He also remarked that he would prefer a school that devoted half time to industrial training.

Discussion: There are no unusual factors in the above case, except that the boy was committed to a reform institution at the tender age of 11 years. His home background is free from antisocial influences, but the Americanization process has not gone far in the parents. His delinquency history shows the influence of a gang. His own appraisal of the educational system is pertinent—he would now prefer for his children a school that devoted half time to industrial training.

Case No. 21—Benedetto O. was born in Italy in 1908, and is now 20 years old. He is at present living at home with his parents. Since last spring he has been working with his father, who is a mason.

His parents came from Northern Italy in 1908, bringing him as an infant. They have not been in want since there is no evidence of their ever applying for relief to any agency.

The father worked as a mason earning $50 a week.

In 1923, they were living in 3 rooms, paying $17 rent. They lived at that address for 8 years and were well spoken of by the neighbors.

The mother, in addition to raising the 3 children, later on undertook to supplement her husband's earnings by doing the janitor work in the tenement.

They then had 6 rooms, but only used 3 for the other 3 were used as a storage place.

The mother's and father's knowledge of English was very limited, and the children soon left them behind. They came and went at will, never informing the parents of their outside life.

A younger brother and sister constitute the rest of the family. This boy, too, did not like school. He and Benedetto do not stay home except to eat and sleep, and keep the parents ignorant of their doings.

There is no definite information concerning the sister, who by now is old enough to work.

Benedetto came to the attention of the Children's Court in 1923, when he was 15. He showed a dislike for school and got in with bad company that led him to play truant. His marks in conduct were C and D. He was sent to Truant School in May, 1920 and kept there until the following March. He was recommitted in October, 1921, and discharged May, 1922.

His parents tried to get him to attend school, but he refused to obey. He repeated his third year in school, 3A and 3B, five terms. During that period he was caught breaking a gas meter and was put on probation.

His intense dislike for school, plus the pressure from his parents, led him to desert his home for a while. He associated with bad boys and admitted entering buildings with intent to steal.

In 1923, when he was examined, a physical test showed him fairly well developed and well nourished. He had enlarged tonsils and a hernia condition, the left testicle being undescended. His tendon reflexes were exaggerated, and he also suffered from nocturnal enuresis. All this suggested a glandular deficiency.

A mental test showed him to be decidedly retarded. Though he was 15 years old, he only reached a mental level of 9 years, 4 months, with an I. Q. of 65 which placed him in the defective class. He was very unstable, sullen, and lazy. At that time he told the medical examiner that his reason for stealing was that he gambled. He also admitted smoking 4 cigarettes a day, and that the movies had a great attraction for him.

Nevertheless, his stay at the Truant School seemed to steady him, for on his return to school he complied with all the requirements and received A in conduct. He left school after reaching the 7A grade.

In 1927, when interviewed by the visitor from this Sub-Commission, he appeared a bit defiant and refused to discuss his former errors, saying that he had nothing to say and that the past was the past.

He is at present earning $4 a day and is learning to be a mason under his father's supervision. He expects to earn more when he knows the trade. He admits now that education is necessary. He often stays away from home in the evenings, going to "certain places" as he terms it, but would not divulge either to his parents or the visitor just what the "certain places" are.

Discussion: Five years ago, at the age of fifteen, this boy was found to have a glandular disturbance and his conduct bore the characteristic behavior symptoms of that type of disease—emotional instability, sullenness and torpidity. He was unfortunately too old for school supervision, consequently no treatment was undertaken. A complete medical service for truants would have detected this case of endocrine disturbance in school life, during the years when glandular therapy could have been consistently carried out and regularly checked up.

Case No. 22—George D., age 20, lives at home, and works as a truck driver. He is keeping steady company with a girl of his own faith. He has no criminal record.

The father, age 45, was born in Italy and came to the United States in 1903. He is in good health, is employed nights as a carwasher in a garage, and earns $35 a week. He is illiterate. In 1926, he was accused of the theft of tires, but the case was discharged in the Magistrate's Court.

The mother, age 39, born in Italy, has been in the United States 24 years, since 1904, and married here. She has been occupied with home duties, is anemic and nervous. She cannot read or write, speaks very little English, but converses intelligently in Italian. She always had to manage the household on an inadequate income, and still feels the pinch of poverty. Her attitude toward the children has not been intelligent or understanding. She has no sympathy for their short-comings or handicaps and has been disposed to rid herself of responsibility. She has been somewhat harsh and inconsiderate of certain needs, such as that of more privacy for her growing daughters.

The family life appears in general to be normal. The group of 7 persons, parents and 5 children have lived for 15 years in cramped quarters, 3 rooms, on the 5th floor of a congested tenement. The home is airy, neat and clean. The neighborhood itself is very poor, and is well known, according to probation officers, for its juvenile gangs, thieves, and children beyond the control of their parents.

The oldest girl, 18, is employed as a dressmaker, at $18. She graduated from Elementary school and attended Manhattan Trade school. She dresses neatly, uses good English and appears to be above average in intelligence. She is engaged to be married.

The youngest girl, age 16, is also a dressmaker, earning $18. She is quiet in manner.

A boy, age 13, is in a Sanitorium, suffering with tuberculosis.

The youngest child, age 11, is in the Catholic Protectory on a delinquency charge, preferred by the mother. This child was ill-behaved in school, being inattentive and disobedient. He once threatened a monitor with a razor not to tell on him. He is not retarded, being in grade 5B. His home supervision was lax; he stayed out late evenings, sometimes until midnight. He stole money at home and divided it with his companions. He attended church irregularly.

The mother, in making the original complaint, hoped he would be placed under supervision among good children and was disappointed when he was returned to her, on probation.

The child's statement is that he doesn't know why he disobeys his mother, and he believes it is a sort of *habit* with him to do so. He says that when he remains at home after school, his mother is forever sending him up and down the stairs, 5 flights, on errands. He would be willing to go if he could make one trip of it. He admits taking money. He was committed to the Protectory for failing to adhere to the terms of probation.

George was born September, 1907. His developmental history is not known. His school record shows retardation amounting to seven terms. He spent 5 terms in the 1st grade, 4 terms in 5A and 2 in 6A. His proficiency ranged from B to C, but his conduct usually was A. He is described as having been skillful in writing compositions. He was untidy, and spent his spare time on the street. When interviewed in 1927, by the field visitor for this Sub-Commission, he gave an unusual cause for his school maladjustment.

It seems that he was a stammerer, and in school was made fun of by his classmates, when called upon to recite. His teachers were not considerate of him, because he took up so much time in reciting. Therefore, although he knew his subjects, the teachers, hard-pressed for time, made him take his seat without reciting. He did not stammer at home, and therefore won no sympathy there. Nor did his mother recognize the need of speech treatment or of psycho-therapy. She expected him to attend, in spite of the handicap. He therefore lost all interest, although he liked school, and played truant. In December, 1920, at the age of 13, he was committed to the Truant school for a period of 6 months. Here he stated, his speech impediment again was a stumbling block. While there, a matron picked him and several other boys to do errands and as recompense gave them pieces of bread and butter or jam, or other sweets. As he could never say "Thank you" promptly she thought him disrespectful, mistreated him, and complained of his behavior. In consequence of this and other minor acts he was transferred to the Catholic Protectory.

He now no longer stutters and says he cured himself of it by refusing to be bothered by the jibes of others. He states that he had many fights over the defect, and believes he would have never been in any difficulty had it not been for it.

He is now a truck driver, and gets along well, according to the statements of himself and his mother. However, in 1926, when his mother referred the younger boy to the Court, she stated that George was away from home and was wild. He has no court record, except for a minor traffic violation in December, 1927.

Discussion—In this case, a serious speech impediment seems to have been a contributing factor in truancy. It is impossible to determine to what extent it was responsible for his numerous retardations, but it is likely he would have experienced difficulty even without it, as his number of retardations is not to be explained on the basis of speech defect alone.

The tragic thing about the case is that no one seemed to realize the functional nature of the stutter. When he was at home he did not stutter. When he stood tongue-tied in school he was dismissed as a dunce and consequently ridiculed by his classmates. Every unfortunate device for reminding him of his affliction was made use of. It was not until he determined to disregard the affliction did it display its functional nature by disappearing. Had this boy had adequate psychotherapy at an early school age it would probably have been unnecessary for him to discover by trial and error a method of over-coming the handicap and much of his conduct difficulties might have been avoided.

Case No. 23—Aaron W., age 21, lives at home and works irregularly, but contributes nothing despite the utter want of his mother and brothers. Private welfare agencies subsidize the family. He has no adult police record.

The father, born in 1880 in Russia, of Hebrew faith, came to the United States in 1909, 3 years after marriage. He suffered from a cardiac condition. He was illiterate, and worked as a cloak operator. He was not a citizen. His death occurred in 1918.

The mother, born in Russia in 1888, of Hebrew faith, came to the United States in 1912. She was at home until the death of her husband, then worked as a scrubwoman. She was unequal to the responsibilities imposed on her, sought to rid herself of the children by committing them to orphanages, dramatized her sufferings, and in other ways showed neurotic behavior. Welfare agencies have refused to institutionalize her children, and she has been granted a small subsidy.

The family always lived on the lower East Side. The present home, lived in for a number of years, consists of four rooms, fairly clean but poorly furnished. The bedroom is dark. Rent, in 1923, was $19.

The family life has been quarrelsome and decidedly unpleasant. Moral standards have been fair.

There are 3 children.

The second child, born in 1914, had measles, whooping cough, chicken pox. In 1915 he had infantile paralysis, which left one leg lame, and caused defective sight and hearing. He has an intelligence quotient of 73, and is in an ungraded class at school. He presents no behavior problems, is well behaved, and puts forth good effort. His teacher states that although he cannot do many things, those things he does are done well. She attributes his backwardness to his handicap and not to innate dullness. The mother tried very hard to place this child in an orphanage, but would not cooperate in securing an X-ray of the child's skull, requested by the institution in question.

The third child, born in 1916, was frail, undernourished, and suffered from bronchitis. His I. Q. was 82, indicative of dull intelligence.

Aaron, born in 1907 in Russia, and now 21, is the oldest. His health has been given a good deal of attention, because of a heart condition he had. As a child, he was underweight, and was granted extra nourishment at a clinic. In 1927, his condition was diagnosed at a hospital as slight functional disease of the heart, anemia and nervous condition. His adenoids and tonsils have been removed.

His school record was satisfactory for both work and conduct. He did not become a truant until the 5B grade, and then was regular in attendance again until 7B.

He was said to spend his spare time on the street and in the movies.

He attended religious school and was confirmed, but has not attended services since.

In 1921, he was in difficulties with his mother, and at her request, a child guidance agency undertook to supervise his spare time. He was urged to join a settlement club, but refused. In school, his truancy led to a transfer to the probationary school. In March, 1922, he was committed to the Truant school, where he remained 4 months, and was graduated.

He has been delinquent twice. In 1920, he stole from a mailbox a letter containing a $30 money order, and had been brought to Court by the American Express Company. The disposition of the case is not known. In January, 1922, he was arraigned in Children's Court on a burglary charge, and placed on probation.

He had learned no trade, despite opportunities offered by welfare agencies, and upon graduation worked irregularly at casual occupations. He said his preference was to be a driver. He made practically no contribution to the home. He frequently left home, impelled by wanderlust. He ran away in the summer of 1923 and again in December, 1925. He and some friends had decided to cross the United States, with California as a goal.

In December, 1927, his mother and he were interviewed by the field visitor of this Sub-Commission.

The mother drew attention to her own pitiable lot, and contrasted with it the easy-going unconcern of her son, who was asleep, although it was nearly noon. She stated that the boy always lacked ambition, but she believes, from what he says, that he is beginning to realize just how limited a future he now has. She was bitter over his non-acceptance of financial responsibility, and stated he was now unemployed and contributing nothing. She believes he is honest, has heard no reports to the contrary, but knows nothing of what he does when out of the house. He eats at home part of the time and buys his own clothing. He leaves on long hiking trips and does not write to her, but returns when he is ragged and penniless.

She blamed herself in part for the strangeness that had grown up between them, saying she is very nervous and "talks out her heart."

The boy, who refused to get up, was interviewed in his room. He spoke civilly, and told the visitor that his mother knew nothing of his conduct or employment, since he tells her nothing. He stated he is qualified to drive a truck or taxi and has a commercial license. He explained his late hours of sleeping, stating he had a temporary night Postoffice job, shifting mail sacks, that would last during the Christmas rush. He rejected the suggestion that permanent work could be secured for him, and said with quiet decision that he could find his own jobs.

The visitor was of the opinion that the mother is overstressing her son's lack of support for fear welfare agencies will withdraw their subsidies.*

Discussion—This boy of neurotic tendencies has refused to accept any responsibility for his mother and brothers, although he is the only possible wage-earner, and allows the family to subsist on a slender charity budget. His behavior, illustrative of a large group of mental cases, constitutes a real problem to the community. Legal steps to force him into working are impracticable and psychiatric treatment at a clinic is out of the question because of his negativism. There is a great need for psychiatrically trained social workers who can carry out effective home treatment among cases such as this.

Case No. 24—Arthur H. is now 18. He lives at home, works more or less irregularly, contributes all of his earnings, attends church regularly and is considered a good boy. He has no police record.

The father, born in the United States, is an unskilled laborer. He has worked as a driver, stableman, and longshoreman. He is employed irregularly, and his income has been inadequate for a family of 10 people. He is employed in a stable at night, earning $25.00 a week. During 1927, he was unemployed for 6 months, and the family was in desperate circumstances. His health is apparently good.

The mother, born in the United States, has always taken care of her home. She has supplemented the family income in recent years by acting as janitress for the tenement house in which they

---

*As this report went to press, a social service agency reported that Aaron had been implicated in a case of assault and robbery and was being held for examination.

live. She is untidy and unclean personally, but affable and apparently in normal health. She is a poor housekeeper and allows her children to go dirty. She has been given some instruction in home hygiene.

The home is in a 4-story tenement house on the West Side, a block from the Hudson River, on the outer fringe of Greenwich Village. The neighborhood is partly Italians, partly Irish, and partly cosmopolitan villagers. Factories and warehouses form the river buildings. A large playground and park occupies a square block around the corner from the house. The family has lived in the same neighborhood for at least 12 years, of which ten years have been spent in the quarters now occupied. These quarters consist of 4 rooms on the top floor (at $12 a month, reduced rental, in lieu of salary for mother's janitor service). The halls which Mrs. H. is supposed to clean, are dirty and dark. The field visitor for this Sub-Commission reports that the kitchen was dark, crowded, and although it was mid-winter, as many flies were buzzing around as on a summer day. The flat is gas illuminated. The rooms are too few in number for the size of the family and there is even a lack of proper sleeping quarters.

The home life is apparently congenial. Big Brothers supervising the boys, and clinic nurses, as well as the present field visitor, were all impressed with the happy family life. The siblings:

James, born in 1906, is now 21. He has been a taxi driver. He is not living at home, and he was not mentioned by his mother when she was interviewed. In 1924, he was reported by a welfare agency as married and working in a market. He has been arrested for several offenses. In 1917, at the age of 11, he stole chickens from a crate on a wagon. He was placed on probation in the Children's Court, but was unco-operative with the Volunteer Big Brother.

In September, 1925, at the age of 19, he was arraigned on a burglarly charge, which was dismissed in the Magistrate's Court. In December, 1925, he was charged with striking another person with his fist. This complaint was dismissed. The same month he paid a fine in Traffic Court for driving without lights. In March 1926, he is recorded as having been given 30 days in the Workhouse for violation of probation. There is no record of the offense itself.

Leslie, born 1912, is now 15. He has been an errand boy, but is often idle. He attends Continuation School. He is on probation to the Children's Court, having stolen $114 worth of women's wear in 1926. His mother states that he has always been a source of trouble, hating school and playing truant. He has been recently released from Truant School. He wants to drive a truck, and claims he cannot find other employment. He is tall, 5 ft. 8 in. The visitor felt he was dull.

There are six other children, ranging in age from 12 years to 19 months. A 7th child died November, 1927, of convulsions. The youngest child is markedly delayed in speech.

Arthur's developmental history is normal, save for scarlet fever and scabies. His school record, except for attendance, was average.

He graduated grammar school at 14, and had 6 months at high school. His conduct was A and B, and his work A and B. He was irregular in attendance from the time he entered school. In October 1920, he was sent to the Truant School for 3 months, while in grade 5-B. He was considered untruthful. Arthur's mother was anxious to have him finish high school, but "he was anxious to get to work so he could have better clothes."

There is no record of a psychological examination on him. His interests, while an adolescent, were few. He belonged to the boys club at the parish church, went out only occasionally with boy friends, attended church regularly on Sundays and enjoyed the services.

He has no trade. His employment history shows no tendency to self-improvement. He worked in a paper box factory, and as wagon helper. He has changed employers frequently. Five different jobs are recorded, and many are undoubtedly un-recorded. In Continuation School, he signed up for auto shop, but habits of truancy persisted, and he was absent 48 out of 92 days. In 1926, he was offered employment by the Big Brother but would not go to his office to be interviewed. His present behavior, as indicated, at the outset, is favorable.

Discussion—Arthur H., coming from a slatternly and impoverished, but congenial home was quite average in his behavior and interests. He was happy-go-lucky and mildly irresponsible, both at school and at work. His career follows that of his forbears, it is utterly lacking in viciousness but is lax, untroubled and ambitionless.

Case No. 25—Ernesto A. is 21, an adult and married. He has married an Italian girl, and is on bad terms with his family, who were not consulted in the matter He has no police record.

His parents were born in Spain, coming here in 1910, when Ernesto was 4 and his younger brother, Pasquale, an infant.

The father obtained work as a stableman at small pay. He continued at this employment for many years until crippled by chronic rheumatism. He is now able to work only 3 or 4 days a week, earning $5 a day, and it is expected that he will shortly become totally incapacitated. He is not a citizen.

The mother cared for her household and children. Her health was good. In 1922 she adopted a 3 year old Spanish child.

In 1918, the family lived in 2 rooms, having only the bare necessities, and paid a rental of $9.50 a month. The father still worked as a stableman, and earned $18 a week. In 1922 they lived in 4 comfortably furnished rooms which were kept clean and tidy.

The parents bore a good reputation among the people whom they knew in the neighborhood.

Pasquale, the younger son, is 15. In 1924, he was placed on probation in the Children's Court for stealing an overcoat. In 1925, he had been twice in the Magistrate's Court for boisterous conduct and crap-shooting with the gang on the block. In 1927, when the visitor from this Sub-Commission interviewed the family, he was in the work-house, having been sentenced to 3 months imprisonment for stealing an automobile.

A medical examination at the work-house revealed that Pasquale is suffering from a venereal disease.

He is not considered really criminally inclined, according to the Detective Bureau which gave its report on the family. Since then he has returned from the work-house, and has been to see the Welfare Lieutenant at the Precinct-house about a job.

Ernesto entered school in this country in 1912; the language was strange, and progress was slow at first. He spent 2 terms in 1A. In Grade 2 he spurted and made both terms in 6 months. In both 3A and 4A he was retarded 3 times, and at the same time his conduct fell from B to C. His attendance was erratic. In 2A and 2B he was present every day; the following term he was away 20 full days; then followed better attendance in the succeeding term. Behavior was even more erratic, ranging from A to D.

He was not a well child. He complained of heart pains and was underweight. He was brought to Bellevue Hospital, examined, and placed on a special diet that included plenty of rich milk.

He made his first communion, but would not attend services, except irregularly when forced by his mother.

He associated with bad company, and his pal was a child who was known to steal. He played long hours on the street, and remained at the movies until 11 p. m. He became friendly with a man who made cheap red wine in a cellar, where he acted as lookout. He was paid in wine, and the job ended abruptly when he came home very drunk. To discipline him, his father took him to the Children's Court, where he was lectured severely and put on probation.

For the next 2 years he did passable work in school. His conduct was at first A, but dropped each term until it reached D.

In 1920, with a friend, he ran away to Philadelphia and then to Washington, where they were arrested and sent back to New York. Ernesto was brought before the Children's Court for violating his probation, and he was committed to the Catholic Protectory.

In 1922 he was brought before the Bureau of Attendance for being absent 22 days in one term, when he was given a second institutional experience, this time at the Truant School, with his parents' consent. Continued truancy brought him back to the bureau, and this time he was committed to the Catholic Protectory. After 2 months there he was discharged as over age.

Prior to the last truancy committment, he spent his nights away from home. During the summer months he slept in hallways. The neighbors said he associated with the worst boys on the block.

On his 16th birthday his father took him back to the Children's Court, and on his last day as a minor, under the laws of New York State, he was returned to the Catholic Protectory. His excuse to the judge was that he hated school, wanted to work and ran away from home because there was no other way out.

When freed, he secured a job as an office boy in a paint office, earning $9 a week.

By 1925, he had acquired a knowledge of automobiles, and was driving a truck. In that year he paid a fine for driving without lights. He has good references from a storage company, for whom he drove an armored car, and carried a pistol. He also worked for a city department, driving a bus. At present he is driving a lumber truck, earning only $25 a week.

He needs money. His wife will give birth to a baby in a month, and Ernesto is still paying doctor bills for a miscarriage she had. He hopes for a good job so he may have his wife and his parents live together. His father will die from heart disease unless he quits work, he is certain. He talks bravely, but the visitor thinks perhaps he is weakening under the strain of family responsibility. Perhaps he hopes to throw part of it on his parents. The visitor is not impressed with him, thinking him mentally deficient and defiant.

Summary: The case of Pasquale is one of a number in which disinterest in school, and resulting conflict with teachers and parents created a tense situation which ended as soon as the boy was free to go to work.

Case No. 26—Fred G., 22, lives at home and works as a truck driver. He assisted his brother, who ran a "speak-easy" in the home neighborhood until it was closed. He has had no police record since 1920.

The parents were born in Italy and came to the United States in 1897. There are 5 children, 4 boys and a girl.

The father, about whom nothing is known, died in 1910.

The mother, age 43, was in severe straits on the death of her husband. She remarried, but the children could not get along with the step-father and she put him out of the house. She worked away from home as a dressmaker, earning in 1917, $2 a day. The children were unsupervised, ran around on the streets and got into much mischief. She gave the impression of not being much concerned over their street behavior. In 1919 she was fined for violating the compulsory education law. She is now a sick woman, complains of headaches and loss of memory for recent events. She acts as janitress and pays no rent. She claims to have made a trip to Italy last year.

The home in 1917 was a clean, well-furnished four-room apartment in a tenement house, renting for $16. The family has been in the same neighborhood for many years, having lived in 6 different places. In 1927, 3 clean and very well-furnished rooms were occupied, in the same block lived in, in 1917.

Two sons are married. An older son has a police record as a safe-blower, and has recently been in the Trenton Prison for carrying a gun. He more recently ran a speak-easy, which was closed.

The youngest son, born in 1908, had borderline intelligence and an I. Q. of 80. He played truant often, going chicken-stealing in

Long Island City. In 1917, he drove an express wagon away from the Long Island depot, was arraigned in the Children's Court and committed to the Catholic Protectory. When examined at the Court Clinic, it was predicted he would become a confirmed offender. His subsequent history has not borne this out, as he has no police record.

Fred was born in July, 1905, in New York City, is 22. His developmental history is not known. He ran the streets, unsupervised, with a gang of youngsters who stole everything that was not nailed; clothes off clotheslines, pigeons, and merchandise from vehicles. They also held up other little boys and took whatever they could find.

Fred was a truant throughout school life, but was not a serious problem until he reached 4th grade. His academic progress was poor. His work ranged from B to C, and he was retarded 5 terms. In 5B, alone, he spent 3 terms. He reached the 6A grade.

In February, 1920, he was committed to Truant School. In all, he was there three times, being discharged on his 16th birthday, in July, 1921.

His reaction to the experiences there were obtained in an interview in 1927. He stated that his first truancy arose over a quarrel at home, when he was not given his school lunch. The truant school was a jail, not a school, he declared. "The only thing they do is keep you there." He believed he was worse when he came out than when he went in because of the evil companions he met there.

In December, 1920, before his last commitment, he was arrested for stealing a horse and wagon from his employer. He gave his age as 16½ and was tried in the adult court. He was placed on probation, and ordered to make restitution of $41. He failed to make payments and a bench warrant was issued, but no action was taken on it.

He was interviewed, in December, 1927. He is single and lives at home. He stated he was working as a truck driver, but refused to state where he worked or what he earned. The police consider him to be a bad youngster and say he has "hung out" in his brother's speak-easy until it was closed.

Summary: A thoroughly poor home environment gave Fred G. a long tether. The father was dead, the mother was lax and indifferent and an older brother was a criminal. Fred himself belonged to a thieving gang. To overcome these handicaps he was sent to an institution, where according to his own retrospection, he was only kept as in a jail, among boys whom he claims made him worse than he previously had been.

MALADJUSTED GROUP

Case No. 27—William B., aged 19, is serving a 3-year term in the Orange County Penitentiary, having been sentenced April, 1927, for escaping the previous year from the New York City Reformatory, where he was serving an indeterminate sentence for pocketbook snatching.

The father, aged 50, was born in Italy. He worked at a variety of occupations which brought in an insufficient income. In 1911, when his family first came to the attention of a welfare agency, he was working irregularly and earning an average of $7 a week. In 1919, he was a longshoreman, at $30 a week. In 1922, he was a peddler at $20 a week, and in 1923, he was in the building trades at $35 a week. In 1927 he was in an accident and spent several weeks in the hospital, suffering from brain concussion. He has his first papers.

The father, it is claimed by detectives who know the family, was the direct cause of his children's delinquencies. When they were young, he taught them to get up early in the morning and steal "market bags," which they later sold in the markets. When they brought money home they were praised, otherwise they were beaten. He had no police record, except for a fine in 1922, for peddling without a license.

The mother, age 41, has taken care of her own household, rearing 7 children. She is in good health. When the family was first known to welfare agencies, in 1911, the mother took good care of the children, and kept her 3-room home neat. In 1913, the two oldest children were brought from Italy and boarders were kept. The mother could not keep up with the added responsibilities, and reports were made that the home was dirty and untidy, the children's clothing ragged, and that they were often kept out of school for want of clothing. The mother showed unwillingness to take advice regarding the medical needs of the children, and was also characterized as lax in her control over them. She is illiterate.

The family lived in a congested, unsanitary East Side neighborhood, 9 persons occupied 3 poorly ventilated and dark rooms, for which in 1922, they paid $10 a month.

There are seven children.

The oldest boy, age 20, is a taxi chauffeur. He has been troublesome since boyhood. He was a truant, a member of a boy's gang, sold newspapers in the subway, frequented movies, and was irregular in church attendance. He was arraigned 4 times as a juvenile delinquent. Once, he caused $50 damage to a school door, shattering the glass with a stone, when refused admittance to the vacation playground because he was too old for the group. On other occasions he stole wool from a showcase and electric bulbs from the passenger platform of an "L" structure. His fourth arraignment was for illegal street selling of newspapers. He has been a chauffeur since 1923. He was arraigned 3 times in Traffic Court for minor violations, and twice for speeding, drawing a $25 fine in 1926 on this charge.

In 1927 he was arrested in Buffalo charged with the theft of an auto in Brooklyn. He received a suspended sentence in a New York Court. In December, 1927, he was arrested on the charge of robbery with a gun, and is now in the Tombs awaiting trial.

The 16-year-old boy has likewise been a truant, a gang member, and a juvenile delinquent. In 1923, he was charged with stealing, in the company of other boys, a roll of cotton goods from a pushcart. He has been fairly helpful to his parents. He spent his spare time tending a push-cart, receiving $4 a week, which he contributed to the family. When his mother was ill, he did the housework. He attended church regularly. In 1926, he ran away from home, and his whereabouts were not known when the family was last heard from.

The 14-year-old child is not known to agencies. He has been put at work in his free time. Once he was chased by a policeman for peddling matches.

Little is known of the girls. The oldest girl, 28, is backward and in ill health, having had 2 attacks of typhoid fever in Italy. A younger girl, now 25, was a school truant.

William, born 1909, is now 19. Nothing is known of his developmental history. His family background and upbringing have already been referred to. His intelligence is retarded, his Binet-Simon I. Q. being 75, on the 16-year adult basis.

His school record shows that he made a fair beginning, but gradually became careless in his work, a conduct problem and a truant. He passed every class until reaching the 4-B grade, which he repeated, doing the same in 5-A and 5-B. His work and conduct dropped to C and D. He was said to smoke and gamble, spent his spare time on the streets, and was indifferent to praise and blame.

In June 1920, he was sent to the Truant School for 4 months, and in April 1921, for 7 months. In 1922, he struck a girl monitor and was sent by the Children's Court to the Catholic Protectory. Here he remained 13 months and reached the 8th grade.

Upon leaving school, he worked very little, but loafed with friends of similar bent.

He has been confirmed and occasionally attended church.

In 1925, just before his 16th birthday, he was arraigned in Children's Court on the charge of breaking a plate glass window, but was discharged. In April, 1925, he was charged with snatching a woman's pocketbook, and sentenced on a Grand Larceny charge to the New York City Reformatory. His date of release is not given, but in December, 1925 he was again arrested on a similar charge. In February 1926, he was again sentenced to the Reformatory on a Grand Larceny charge. He made a successful escape, but in April, 1926 was captured and sentenced to the Orange County Penitentiary for 3 years on the charge of jailbreaking.

Since the age of 11, this nineteen-year-old boy has spent nearly five years in truant schools, reformatories, jail and prison.

He was examined physically in 1927, found to be temperate in habits, not a user of drugs, and in fairly good general condition.

Mentally, he is retarded, with 12-year intelligence and fair mechanical ability. He is thought to have sufficient industrial capacity to earn a living should he wish to. But he is considered as having a psychopathic personality, and therefore presents a poor prognosis.

Discussion: William B. comes from a home of low moral standards. He is a borderline defective and has a psychopathic personality. He has lived his entire life on the streets, a not unnatural tendency for a child from a home where parents, six brothers and sisters and two boarders all live in three rooms.

Who can have done anything for him? We can eliminate his parents and siblings because of their own backwardness and misbehavior. The school functioned only until the fourth grade; just as soon as his capacity for learning was over-taxed, William lost interest and became a truant. There was no flexibility in the school program to provide him with vocationally useful, yet interesting tasks. In view of his instability, however, his success at such a program would be doubtful.

If we consider the facts frankly, this boy and his whole family would seem to be liabilities instead of assets to the community. A city that measures its multiplication of population in terms of family units such as this has no cause for celebration. Yet under the existing circumstances, William's parents and thousands of their ilk will continue to breed defective, uncared for children.

Case No. 28—Emilio A., born in 1905, now 23, has had an institutional record. He "hangs out" with a crowd of East Harlem men known to the police as former convicts, constantly engaged in "shady" transactions such as dope-peddling and bootlegging. He does not work, as he is seen on street corners at all times of the day.

The parents were born in Italy. There were 6 children. The father, of whom nothing is known, has been dead 17 years. The mother, age 65, has lived in recent years with her two younger sons and a daughter.

She made a meager income by caring for a working neighbor's five children, receiving $1 a week for each. In 1924, being too feeble to continue even this, her children allowed her to be placed in the City Home for the Aged on Blackwell's Island. The mother, when she maintained a home, was said to be a good housekeeper, but was totally ignorant of what went on outside of the house and knew nothing of the daily lives of her sons.

The family lived for 12 years in the same neighborhood, a congested portion of East Harlem, near the East River, in 3 rooms, paying $12.50 rent. The neighborhood is described by court investigators as being rife with crime, drug addiction, and sex degeneracy.

Two sisters are married. A brother, now married, was arraigned in Children's Court for some petty matter when a boy. Another brother is a plasterer. The youngest daughter remained at home, helping with the housework until the home was broken.

Emilio, the youngest child in the family, went to grammar school until grade 8A. His conduct was fair and work was poor. There was no record of truancy is grammar school.

In February, 1920, he went to work in a Long Island shoe company as a clerk at $15 a week. He remained until September and left of his own accord, his work being satisfactory. He was idle a while, and then claims to have worked for a Manhattan printer for 3 months, earning $2. This has not been verified.

In 1920, he was arraigned in the Magistrate's Court and given a suspended sentence for maintaining live pigeons on the roof. In December, 1920, he was committed to Truant school for failing to attend Continuation school. In 1921, he was arraigned twice again on the same charge and was recommitted, remaining until March, 1922.

In May, 1922, he was charged with sodomy on an eleven year old boy, convicted on a disorderly conduct charge, and sent to the New York City Reformatory. Here his record was bad; he fought with keepers and inmates, was insolent and refused to work.

He was paroled in January, 1924, and went to live with an older sister. Here he was not tolerated because of his shiftless habits. He was said to keep bad company and loafed in poolrooms. His brother-in-law shielded him, however, by telling the parole officer that Emilio worked for him, when he was unemployed. In April, the boy disappeared, and was not heard of until September when caught speeding in a stolen auto. He pleaded guilty to Attempted Grand Larceny, second degree, was given a suspended sentence, and returned to the Reformatory for violation of parole, remaining until May, 1925.

He stated that from April to September, 1924, he worked in Boston as a waiter, for several weeks for the I. R. T., and then at odd jobs.

Since his release, he associates with ex-convicts and does not work.

Discussion: Until this boy got into difficulties over truancy from Continuation school, his record was ordinary. He reached the 8th grade and was not a truant. Then came three truancy commitments, a commitment for sodomy and another for auto theft.

This young man's career raises several pertinent questions. There are indications of idleness, truculence and sex abnormality beginning with adolescence. No mental examination was ever given to determine whether here was a beginning psychosis. His sex abnormality followed three institutional commitments. There has been no inquiry into what experiences antedated this behavior.

Both of these questions should have been answered by those responsible for his various incarcerations. If his is a developing psychosis, then he is in need of expert medical care. If he is normal mentally, then we still have facing us the unpleasant reality that institutional treatment made him, not better, but worse.

Case No. 29—William S., age 18, has learned no trade, and works as an errand boy, irregularly. He shows no enthusiasm for vocational schooling. He is now home, nursing a wound in the leg, and will not tell how he came by it.

The father, born in the United States, of Negro descent, has lived in New York City 6 years. He is uneducated, and was a longshoreman. In 1922, he fell from a ladder and since then claims to be ill, although at the time of the accident he was able to go home unaided, after receiving ambulance treatment for bruises. He was working in 1925, earning $40 a week.

The mother, of Negro descent, was born in the Unitel States, and has been in New York 6 years. She is in good health, is uneducated.

In 1922, shortly after coming North, she was fined for keeping an unmuzzled dog.

The home, consisting of 6 rooms, renting for $40, is plainly furnished, but neat. The neighborhood is poor and congested.

The family belong to a Methodist congregation.

There are five children.

The oldest, born in 1900, a laborer, has been twice arrested and fined, in 1920 and in 1921 when he first came North, once on a disorderly conduct charge and once on a charge of Attempted Felonious Assault. He is married.

The history of the others is not known.

William, born August, 1909, is now 18. He came North with his parents at the age of 12. His developmental history is not known. When he entered school, he was placed in the 1B grade. The first term he was absent 44 days, but attendance subsequently improved. His work and conduct were very inferior, and he was described as inattentive, and fond of fighting and annoying others.

He spent most of his free time with a gang that "hung out" on the docks at the Harlem River. Here they swam, loafed, and planned stealing escapades. He frequently stayed away from home for days at a time, with his gang friends, who were said to have great influence over him.

In April, 1921, during his first year North, he was sent to the Truant school, remaining 3 months. In November, 1921, he was recommitted, remaining until September, 1922. He reached only the 3B grade.

In July, 1925, he was arraigned in the Children's Court charged with stealing a bundle of cigarettes in cartons from a wagon, in company with his gang. He was placed on probation, with the understanding that he was to be sent South to relatives. This, it was thought, was the only way of detaching him from the gang, as he stated very definitely that he didn't care to remain at home and would run away at the first opportunity.

He was sent South, but apparently did not remain long, as in October, 3 months later, he was arrested for making improper suggestions to a school girl. He was placed on probation in the Children's Court.

Two months later, he was arrested for pushing his way without paying through a subway turnstile. He gave his age as 18, and was placed on probation in the Magistrate's Court.

In December, 1927, the house was visited by a field visitor for this Sub-Commission. The visitor's report is as follows:

"Found the mother at home ironing. The father is sick in bed— he has never been all right since the flu and a fall he had some 5 years ago from a ladder. William had been home for about 2 weeks with a wound in his leg. One could get no definite information as to the cause of the accident.

"William has been a fairly good boy since his release from Truant school. He has been working as errand boy in a hat shop and went out for a job to-day. When he works he brings his pay envelope home, and hands all he earns over to his mother.

"'No! I couldn't say where he goes when he's not home after work, nor what kind of friends he have, but he do go to church.'

"The mother showed a card for William where he is asked to act as usher on Sunday. Just now the 3 older boys are also out of work. That, coupled with the man of the house being laid up, makes it very hard. The mother does not lecture William, but talks to him and tries to explain things to him, she says. While the mother talked a lot around William, she said very little about the boy himself.

"The mother said that she had had no trouble with the older boys in school and could not account for William's behavior and was going to the Y. M. C. A. to see if it were possible to have William learn a trade. She would be glad if he would go to night school, but he shows no enthusiasm.

"'No! He's not been troublesome and is very good when he is home.'"

Discussion: In this case, there is evidence of a family maladjustment incident to moving from a southern town to a northern metropolis. William's dislike for school is not hard to understand when one notes that his school experience began at 12, in grade 1B of a formal northern class-room. His gang affiliations and the things that he and his companions did for amusement are illustrative of what boys will do when denied normal opportunities for recreation. The portion of Harlem, where William lives, is almost devoid of public or private facilities for recreation.

Case No. 30—Morris K. was born in New York City in 1908 and is now 19 years 5 months. He is at present working as a painter, for one of his older brothers. He lives with his parents and is devoted to them, contributing most of his salary.

The father, a native of Russia, emigrated to this country 24 years ago. By occupation he is a painter, but due to old age and ill health—he is suffering from asthma and hernia,—he has been unemployed for the last 5 years, and is practically dependent upon his children for his maintenance. He is a simple, illiterate individual, who in spite of being devoted to his family, possesses insufficient intelligence to control them properly. He was married to Morris's mother one year after the death of his first wife. The 4 children of the first marriage, ranging in age from 39 to 29, are all married and established in their own homes.

The mother, while illiterate, possesses natural intelligence and appears the dominant factor in the household. She seems to exercise a wholesome influence over the children.

There is no record against any of the members of the family, with the exception of Morris. The children are normally healthy and appear to be well cared for. The oldest daughter, 22, is employed as a bookkeeper. A boy of 16 is attending high school, and the youngest boy, 7, is in public school.

Prior to moving to the Bronx, 2 years ago, they lived for 10 years in the same house in an uncongenial atmosphere in a very congested neighborhood. In 1920, when the family, due to Morris' truancy, became known to a social agency, they were living in 4 rooms at a rental of $16. There was not much income then, the parents seemed unprogressive, the father working irregularly.

At the age of 10, Morris fell from the fifth floor fire-escape to the yard and was confined in the City Hospital for a month; he was unconscious for 3 weeks of that period. The parents stated that since then he has been easily excited and nervous.

He failed of promotion twice in the 2A and 2B grades, and left 3 times in 6B with an average rating of C. In 1920 he became a constant truant and uncontrollable. The mother failed in all her attempts to compel the boy to attend school, and though the father punished him constantly, it was to no avail.

Morris showed a preference for work long before he was of age, and seemed very fond of money. Upon investigation he was found to be employed by a bakery as a helper on a wagon, earning 75c to $1 a day. Being illegally employed, he was returned to school.

In spite of his religious training, it had failed to make any impression on him, and his sense of moral values was defective. In 1919, he was arrested for entering a building and stealing rubber stamps and keys. He was placed upon probation and upon favorable report received a suspended sentence.

In May, 1921, he was accused of accompanying another in a burglary, and in June, 1921, his truancy became pronounced. In December, 1921, he was sent to Truant school, and after an 8 months' stay was returned to public school. After a few days he ran away from home and was located by the police in Newport News, Va. On his return he was placed in a disciplinary school and attended regularly, behaving at home, and retiring early. He even joined the library and seemed to have adjusted himself.

The boy appears mentally defective, yet in general seems to have given satisfactory service to his employers. He worked as errand boy, "pin boy" at a casino, and delivery boy for a laundry, earning from $12 to $20, respectively. He was dominated by the older members of his family and given very little opportunity to think for himself. Possessing low mentality, he was also impressionable and easily influenced. He had been known upon occasions to frequent cheap pool rooms in Harlem, where he came in contact with an undesirable element that had a marked effect on his character.

In 1926, he was indicted for grand larceny, and committed to the reformatory. He feloniously stole and carried away $349, the property of a large department store where he was employed as chauffeur. He was authorized to collect money on delivery of C. O. D. packages. He hid the money in his overcoat at home, and reported to the police that he had been the victim of a hold-up;

but on further examination he confessed he had hidden the money. It appears that he had heard of occurrences similar to the one he attempted in this instance having been successfully perpetrated by other employees of his firm, and so planned this affair.

His family knew nothing of what had occurred until they received notice of his arrest. By now they had moved to a 6 room apartment, paying $50 rent.

In 1927, Morris was examined mentally, and was rated as an "inferior, probably feeble-minded, in the moron class." His I. Q. was 64 and his mental age was 10 years 2 months for a chronological age of 18 years 8 months. "The patient gives impression of being a weak type. Dull normal mentality, reasoning poorly and slowly. Impulsive and weak willed."

Since he was placed on probation, his family has been very cooperative. Morris is employed as a painter for one of the older brothers and receives a salary of $6 a day. He seems to give satisfactory service. The home is comfortably furnished, well kept, and in a neighborhood that presents opportunities for normal pursuits. Morris has started a savings account. He has shown no enthusiasm in an attempt to interest him in attending evening school, nor does he wish to join the Public Library, because he cannot seem to keep his mind on books.

Nevertheless, he contributes most of his money to the home, has bought a radio, using all his spare money to pay off installments, and spends most of his leisure time at the instrument.

Discussion—Morris is an example of what can be done with a feeble-minded boy under half-way normal home circumstances. He is weak-willed and easily influenced, but may be just as easily directed into useful as into harmful ways. He works satisfactorily under friendly direction and is content with simple amusements, such as listening to the radio. And, what is probably most significant, he now lives in a non-congested neighborhood where gang influences are not strong.

Case No. 31—Luigi F. is in the House of Refuge, having been sentenced in September, 1926 on two charges, that of Grand Larceny, and impairing the morals of a minor.

The parents were born in Italy and came to the United States in 1897, bringing one infant. Seven other children were born in New York City.

The father, age 58, has been at various times a cement worker and bricklayer. He is described by the police, who know the family, as being a respectable man, who worked with pick and shovel, all his life. Because of his hard work, he left to his wife the problem of rearing the children. He was ordinarily kind, but when he was appealed to, to discipline the children, he grew hot-tempered and ruled with a heavy hand. He has no police record except for a violation of the compulsory education law, on which sentence was suspended.

The mother, in addition to rearing eight children, did home sewing on overcoats to add to the family income.

The family has lived on the Lower East Side, and in a congested Brooklyn waterfront section. Their present quarters consist of 5 rooms, three of which are dark. The rent is $26 a month. The toilet is in the hall, shared by two families. There is no bath.

There appears to have been little supervision of the children, according to the police. The Bureau of Attendance, however, reports the parental care as "good."

The oldest boy has set a very poor example to the younger children. He reached grade 7A in school. Since 1912, he has been implicated in various offenses. He has been a juvenile delinquent, was arrested for burglary 3 times, was twice discharged, and spent 2½ years in Sing Sing for the third offense. He has been found guilty of disorderly conduct, petty larceny, receiving stolen goods, and unlawful entry. He has been in Elmira Reformatory and in the work-house. In 1920, he was sent to Sing Sing for 7 years for possessing burglar's tools. He was paroled in 1925, and parole expired in December, 1927.

He is now married, is working in a fish market, and is believed by detectives to be "going straight."

Two daughters are married. Two other daughters appear to be mentally slow. One son is in the Army.

Luigi was born in 1909 and is now 16. His developmental history is not known. In 1920, at the age of 11, he had scarlet fever. He complains of a weak back.

His school record shows fair attendance until the fifth grade, when he was truant 22 days out of the term. His work was B plus and B, and his conduct ranged from A to C, but was usually B. He was described as being skillful at all sorts of hand work. He was 3 terms retarded. He used obscene language, stole, told lies, and "was stubborn, at times akin to insanity."

During his spare time he polished shoes.

The impressions of a visiting nurse in 1924, when he was 13, are somewhat similar. She describes him as sullen and stubborn. His parents wanted him to work after school and he objected vigorously.

In May, 1920, at the age of 11, he was committed to the Truant School, remaining until February, 1921. He was returned to school, and remained until 1924, leaving at the age of 15 while in the 8th grade. A Children's Court record at the age of 13 states he was placed on probation for forcing a window and stealing brooms valued at $12. Little is known of his subsequent record. He was irregularly employed as a peddler. The Continuation School he attended reports that in October, 1924 he was a porter in a barber shop, earning $10 a week, and in February, 1926 he was a helper on a truck, earning $15.

In 1925 and 1926 he was arraigned in the Municipal Court for failing to attend Continuation School. In both instances he was placed on probation. In September, 1926 he was held on a charge of picking pockets, and sentenced to the House of Refuge. At about the same time he was found guilty of impairing a minor's morals. Both sentences are to run concurrently.

The detectives who know both Luigi and the older brother believe that neither of them is really vicious, and venture the guess that they might have made good citizens if properly disciplined in childhood.

Discussion: At the age of eleven, Luigi showed signs of a severe emotional disturbance which was aggravated by unwise home discipline. No inquiry was made into the reasons for his sullenness and stubbornness, he was condemned as a "bad" boy and packed off to Truant School. Now, at 16, he is a pickpocket and a sex offender, and the chances of successfully retraining him have diminished to the vanishing point.

In school he was described as skilful in all sorts of hand work. The school curriculum was not adapted to provide vocational training for him, so he turned his skill to the picking of pockets.

The school lost two golden opportunities to train him properly. Had provisions existed for sifting such boys out from the mass, and applying individual treatment, he might be an honest wage-earner today.

Case No. 32—Henry J. was borne in New York City in 1908. He is now 20, and at present living at home. He was paroled from the New York City Reformatory in 1927, having served a term for stealing an auto.

The father came from England 22 years ago, and has been employed as a chauffeur. His attitude towards convention was indifferent, for it was not until Henry's mother had borne him 5 children that he legally married her. He was irregularly employed, and when he did work he would rather spend his money on chorus girls or disappear from home. Thus the family came to the attention of charitable associations. The father's record from 1919 to 1922 was not a very pleasant one, for it covered charges from violations of speed laws, traffic rules, health laws, theft, homicide, nonsupport of family to that of abducting and living with a 16 year old girl. Being frequently away from home, his interest in the children was decidedly negligible; and when in 1923 he deserted the family for good, not having been heard from since, the burden of rearing the family fell on the mother.

The mother was a German Jewess, and came to this country 21 years ago. She is illiterate, weak-willed and of low moral standards, for she lived unconventionally with Henry's father only after a casual acquaintanceship. After her first five children were born, she became converted to Catholicism and in 1918, eleven years after living with the man, they were married by a Catholic priest.

The complete family of 8 children were brought up in the Catholic faith and in spite of regularly attending religious services, very little real impression was made on them.

In 1923, the family of 10 were living in a cramped and impoverished condition in 4 rooms in an old-fashioned tenement, paying a rental of $15. They were kept clean and neat.

Though the mother was quite noisy in correcting the children, she was considered a respectable woman, but burdened with the

responsibility of such a large family, she was incapable of properly guiding their conduct. They were allowed to roam the streets at will and associate with whom they pleased. No trace of the father has been found to the present, and the charities have been supporting the family so as not to break up the home.
The oldest daughter is married now. Two of the younger girls were committed to institutions on charges of parental neglect. They were found on the streets late at night, begging and stealing, and the younger one was subject of a rape. The other children regularly attend parochial school, and nothing outstanding is known of them.
Henry began his education at a parochial school, and later attended the public school. During his scholastic career his record and attendance vacillated between A and D, and his attendance was very irregular. Because of constant truancy, at 15 he was sent to the Truant School for 3 months. Three months later he was recommitted for a period of 8 months. Attaining the grade of 7-A at 15, his educational training ended and he went to work. He was then known as dull, unreliable and untruthful.
His leisure time was spent on street corners with the hoodlums in the neighborhood.
Though his health condition appeared fair, at 15 he was small and undeveloped for his age, and he gave one the impression that he was subnormal. Yet he was alert, fairly intelligent and a good talker.
His work varied from messenger boy, helper on a truck, to that of flag boy for the New York Central Railroad, earning an average of $16, $15 of which he gave to his mother. His employers, when interviewed, recommended him as a steady and useful worker. His constant changing was caused by a preference for outside work and a desire for more wages.
Parental negligence and inability to control his conduct led him to join a noisy, mischievous, drinking crowd, and he soon learned to conduct himself in a disorderly manner.
In 1926, at 18, he and a group of boys of similar age, were arrested for disorderly conduct on a bus outing, and Henry was given 10 days in the Workhouse. He also got in with a bunch of rowdies who made a business of stealing cars, stripping them and selling the parts. In September 1926, he and some others stole a car, damaged it while driving, and on a charge of larceny he was sent to the reformatory. In spite of being found at the wheel driving the car, Henry boldly asserted his ignorance of the purpose, and emphatically denied any connection whatsoever with the actual stealing. He said that he was under the impression it was just a joyride, but the knowledge of his association with such unsavory characters was known to the police and his excuses did him no good. Paroled in 1927, he is living at home. His recent work record could not be obtained.
Discussion: An unfortunate family history, and association with a dishonest gang are the obvious high lights of Henry J.'s career.

Yet another fact is important: He kept changing jobs because he was not satisfied with low wages, and was tempted to join an auto stealing gang because of the profits.

It will be noted that most of the boys in this case study group worked for very low wages. It is of course true that many of them were incompetent to earn high wages in skilled employment, but they were for the most part in good physical health and could do a man's work at rough labor.

A certain well-known welfare worker, who has been an inspiration to thousands of under-privileged boys, refuses to send boys to employers who under-pay on the ground that a job that does not pay an adequate wage cannot keep a boy "going straight."

This theory should be pondered over by employers of young men.

Case No. 33—Timothy C. was born in New York City in 1906. He is now 22 and is living at home with his father, works regularly and contributes $20 a week to the household.

There is no definite knowledge of the parents and the home environment, but it is known that the parents were always self-supporting and had no police record. The mother died in 1926 of pneumonia.

Timothy, an only son, went to public school the first 2 years, truancy playing a part, and was then discharged to a parochial school for 3 years. At 13, he was again transferred to the public school but spent most of the school term loafing on the streets. At 15 he was committed to the Truant School for 2 months, and since that did not improve his attendance, he was again sent there and discharged after a stay of 6 months, when he reached his sixteenth birthday. He reached the 6th grade.

Though his home was considered normal, and his church attendance regular, there was a lack of parental supervision. When examined at the age of 18, he was found to be both physically and mentally retarded. He had no special training and was employed as helper on a truck. In 1924, he was arrested for removing the contents of an open drygoods case from a truck, but was put on probation for 2 years. While on probation he has worked steadily and is considered to have "made good."

Case No. 34—Matthew M. was born in New York City in 1906. He is now 22. In 1926, he was arrested for being found intoxicated in a stolen auto. He was working but living away from home in a furnished room with his mentally deficient brother. He is known as a gangster.

The father came here from Ireland when quite young, and the mother was born in the United States of Irish parents.

The family consisted of 3 children, 2 boys and a girl. In spite of having the 3 children to rear, the mother, who had been a domestic servant before her marriage, occasionally did a day's work to supplement the father's earnings.

The father was a glazier by trade and had very good references, but worked most irregularly and seemed unable to hold a satisfactory position for any length of time. In 1906 a charitable organization was appealed to for relief, as the family had gotten into debt and the father was out of work.

They lived in 2 rooms, at that time, paying $6.50 rent. Later conditions must have been worse for they then occupied a furnished room, paying $2.50 a week. In 1912, the father deserted for a time.

The mother, though coming from a good family, was frail and sickly, slow in learning and very untidy. She had little control over the children and was known to be tricky and unreliable. The home was filthy and badly ventilated. The mother disclosed the fact that the husband was a confirmed drinker and had no desire to work steadily.

In 1921, when Matthew was 15, the father died of alconolism, combined with tuberculosis and heart trouble. He had never been a real contributing factor in the home and was satisfied to have the children committed to institutions so that the responsibility of supporting them could be taken off his shoulders.

The mother since has been working in the capacity of office cleaner, earning $12 a week.

The daughter, who is living away from home now, is a telephone operator. She had been placed with a friend when quite young, at a time when the parents were put out on the street for nonpayment of rent.

The two other children, Matthew and a younger brother, who was a mental defective, grew up without any parental interest or control.

In 1912, when Matthew was six, he was committed to a convent for improper guardianship. In 1918 and 1919, he was arraigned for juvenile delinquency, but placed on parole both times. He associated with gangs, was found hanging around the docks, and frequently brought the gang into the house. Both brothers accused each other of theft several times, and said that the money thus obtained was spent on candies and the movies. In 1921, Volunteer Big Brother supervision was given.

In 1922, at 15, Matthew was sent to the Protectory for truancy and kept there until his sixteenth birthday completing the sixth grade there. Then as soon as the law allowed, he went to work. He earned $15 as a helper, and after a while got a job in a laundry for $21, where he was regarded as reliable, and trusted with money. He worked there for 2½ years and his services were satisfactory.

In 1926, at the age of 20, he and three companions all intoxicated, were arrested for stealing an automobile, presumably with the intention of taking a joy-ride. The court took a charitable view of the case and discharged them after investigating their past records.

For two years prior to his arrest he had attended an industrial class at the settlement house. Though he was untidy in appearance, he was a good worker. He was known for a bully and a tease in spite of his good nature. On a mental examination in 1925, when he was 19, he attained an I. Q. of 80 and a mental age of 12 years three months, which gave him a rating of dull intelligence.

He was known to have stayed away from home nights, and when last arrested he was found living in a furnished room with the younger brother, 17. There was no respect nor love for the mother, for he was also accused of striking her. Most of his time had been spent away from home in institutions. Matthew has the reputation of being a "gangster."

Discussion: In 1921, Matthew M. was given supervision by a volunteer Big Brother assigned by a welfare agency doing volunteer child guidance work. The report by that agency of its contact in 1921 is enlightening in view of the true facts known about the family, as obtained from the records of courts, family case work agencies, and settlements. The Big Brother reported:

"The father, very old, a janitor, is gentle and kindly . . . parents temperate, industrious and of good standards."

After a year and a half, the volunteer gave up the attempt, because the boy was un-cooperative. Having so inadequate a grasp of this family's background, what could one expect of that well-meaning volunteer except failure?

This single case illustrates a point worth emphasizing—that preventive efforts, if they are to be effective, must be made by trained persons, who can size up a family situation accurately, and who can utilize all of the community's resources in studying the individual delinquent and planning for him.

Case No. 35—Philip S. was born in Baltimore, Maryland, in 1906 and is now 22. At present he is out of work but lives with his mother. He stays home during the day, but goes to the movies at night, returning about 11 p. m.

The parents are American born. They came to New York from a small southern town about 20 years ago. The six children, three boys and three girls, were all born in the United States. There is no knowledge of the father's trade, but after his death in 1920, the mother declared that she was able to manage well and did not have to go out to work. From 1917 to 1920, the father had acted queerly, would not trust his wife and had lied to her when she had gone South on a visit. He wrote saying that the children were ill, and on her return he became so violent that it was necessary to send him to the hospital. Four months later he died in an insane asylum.

The mother now lives on the top floor of a three-story commercial building, paying $25 rent for five rooms, and has been living there for the past 15 years. She appeared pleasant toward the visitor from this Sub-Commission, but was extremely evasive and would not touch on any question concerning the delinquency in the family. The home impressed one as harsh and cold.

In spite of giving the impression that her family were in good financial circumstances and of good social standing, she herself was slovenly dressed and unclean. Her hair was badly in need of combing and her teeth were in bad condition. She appears to have no especial interest in the children, saying that she could not be bothered to visit the two older ones who are married.

The younger daughter is on the stage, a chorus girl, and comes home only when she is playing in New York.

One brother is employed as a traveling salesman, and contributes liberally when he works.

Two of the boys besides Philip have records known to the police. From 1918 to 1925 they have been arraigned on charges varying from violations of traffic regulations to theft and counterfeiting. One of them has been an inmate of the House of Refuge and the New York City Reformatory. At the age of 17 he was examined and found to have acute gonorrhea. A mental test at that time showed him to be defective, with an I. Q. of 55 and a mental age of 8 years, 11 months.

Philips school career was the usual one. He progressed steadily to the third year, and his truancy manifested itself in the fourth year. He was retarded twice each term, and the following two years conduct and work graded at B and C. He was very disagreeable and stubborn, and could not be persuaded to attend school regularly.

At the age of 14 he was committed to the Truant school for more than a year. It apparently had very little effect, and his mother complained stating that he wanted to do nothing but lie around and sleep, and she sometimes thought he was not right in the head.

He was too dull to mingle with a gang, but managed to get into trouble, nevertheless. In 1921, at 15, he was arrested for stealing a coat from an automobile, but was discharged on parole. At the age of 16, he was apprehended for burglary, and at that time the examinations made showed him normal physically but defective mentally, with an I. Q. of 66 and a mental age of 10 years one month.

In 1923 he was committed to the House of Refuge for violating probation. His conduct at the institution was fair, and he was never in trouble after his parole. In April, 1926 he disappeared from home and no word from him was had until the supervision of his parole expired.

The mother, when questioned, said that Philip at present is not well, and that he coughs a lot. He is not getting any medical attention as he is very stubborn and she can do nothing with him. No information regarding the type of work he does could be elicited, and the mother would not give any reasons for his truancy. The mother is very shrewd and cleverly blocks any attempt to disclose any real information that might enlighten one as to causes for Philip's condition.

Discussion: The problem of supervising the criminal feebleminded in New York state has never been adequately met, as shown in the case of Philip S.

Commitments to institutions are only temporary, and commitments even to the institution at Napanoch, intended for the permanent segregation of criminal defectives, are usually terminated by parole, because of the crowded condition of that institution.

The case of this young man is a real challenge. He is known to be a truant, a thief and a defective. He is known to have brothers with criminal records. It is known that his mother cannot or will not control him. Yet he is now at large in the community, unsupervised, his period of parole having expired.

His case could be duplicated by hundreds. In the absence of a program of delinquency prevention for truants, there is a great need for continued supervision of young men of this type.

Case No. 36—Isidore B. was born in New York City in 1907. He is now 21, and is at present in the Elmira Reformatory serving a sentence for an unprovoked assault upon an officer in an effort to escape.

The parents came here from Russia 27 years ago in 1901. Their four sons were born in the United States. They do not seem to have been in want, since there is no record of their being financially aided by any social organization. In 1915, the father was working for a slaughter house and was earning enough to provide for the family. The home was kept fairly clean, though they were living in a congested tenement district. There was not much parental control over the children, and no attempt made to better conditions for in 1928 they were found to be living at the same address. The father has changed his mode of work, for he is now employed as a laundry worker earning $30 a week.

Nothing outstanding is known of the mother.

The three younger brothers are known to the police. One of them, a chauffeur, was arrested nine times from 1920 to 1924 for violating traffic rules, speeding, and for assault. Another one, at 16, was apprehended for playing cards, gambling, and disorderly conduct; at present he is in the Army. And the 11 year old was arrested for attempting to steal money from a cash register.

Evidently the oldest boy, Isidore, has influenced their conduct by his actions and perhaps teachings. Isidore showed a dislike for school, beginning with the second grade. He was retarded twice every term in 2-A, 2-B and 3-A, due to his truancy and bad conduct. In 1919, at 12, he had already been twice in the Truant School, preferring it to public school. He wanted to work.

His marks in school varied, his conduct was B and A, and his work went from A to C. In his 5th and 6th years he again was left back twice, and 3 times successively with conduct and work C. He was sent to the Truant School 5 times, and once to the Jewish Protectory.

He had deserted his home several times, and had also taught the younger brother to steal. The school being 7 blocks from home, it seemed too much effort to make the trip, and the gang on the street had a greater attraction. Though he was fond of athletics, he could not be persuaded to join a club. He seemed more adjusted after he was permitted to work. He had no regular employment, working on trucks and when occasion arose removing snow from the streets.

In 1925, at 18, he was arrested for possessing burglar's tools and sent to a reformatory. His conduct at that institution was very bad. A medical examination developed nothing abnormal except flat feet. His mental examination showed a 13-year 2-months level and an I. Q. of 82, while his chronological age was 17 years and 11 months. On this basis his intelligence was dull.

He was in 7-A when he left school and was placed approximately in the same class in the institution.

An unprovoked assault upon an officer in an effort to escape resulted in his being transferred to Elmira Reformatory, where he now is.

Discussion: In Isidore's case the gang had more fascination than the social settlement. The attractiveness of predatory street life over the greater decorum of clubs and settlements makes it particularly difficult to incorporate into well-disciplined groups those children who have tasted freedom and adventure. In a way, the problem epitomizes the struggle between the frontier and civilization.

Time was when the adventurous and the unruly went West. Today, for the unruly, the streets of large cities are the social frontier. The winning of this last frontier is a task to which communities, aided by educators and recreation workers, must bend their energies.

Case No. 37—Peter C., age 21, born in September, 1909, is today an inmate of the New York State Reformatory, having assisted in the theft of $100 worth of shoes from a show window. His history presents behavior problems over a span of 13 years, since the age of eight.

The paternal heredity is normal, but the maternal line shows decided neuropathic tendencies. The grandmother was ill and nervous. An uncle was "notoriously crazy," drank and refused to work. Another uncle drank, abused his family, and then deserted. Two other maternal uncles are feeble-minded inmates of Randall's Island, a municipal institution for mental defectives.

Neither parents have ever been examined, physically or mentally. The father, age 40, gives evidence of fair intelligence. He was born in Italy. During his early married life he was a driver, and in 1917, earned but $18 a week. Subsequently, he has become a foreman for a plasterer contractor, and has profited by the general increase in wages to the building trades, his present earnings ranging from $40 to $75 a week. He is, and always has been, the sole support of the family. He has been in court only once, because of the truancy of his children. He seems to have been a man of good intentions, but possessed traits of hot temper and cruelty, which exhibited themselves in unwarrantedly severe beatings to the children. He was arrogant in disregarding their rights, but in fairness to him, it must be stated that he was probably the only member of the family possessing adequate intelligence, and both found it easy and felt it necessary to over-rule the unintelligent behavior of his offspring.

The mother's history is negative in most respects. She is American-born. She married at seventeen, was a mother at 18, and has raised a family of eight children. Today she is 36. All her years have been spent in the house. Fifteen of them, she has been in the same four-room apartment in a congested tenement. She has been a fair housekeeper, and her home has been described as clean and neat. She is described by a family welfare agency as having been co-operative, but seemed mentally incapable of coping with problems. In view of her unfavorable heredity, and the poor mentality of her children, it is not an unwarranted assumption, that she, too, was retarded in intelligence, if not actually defective.

The home was adequate in size when first occupied in 1911, there being only two infants. Six subsequent births made the 4 rooms congested beyond decency. It was not until 1926 that the family moved to better quarters in the Bronx, at the insistence of a court probation officer.

The siblings have been retarded in their development. May, born in 1913, was a behavior problem child at the age of four. Joseph, born 1910, is feeble-minded, with an I. Q. of 57, and has been recommended for institutional segregation because of truancy and incorrigible behavior. Arthur, born 1912, is in an ungraded class at school.

Peter, the oldest child, was a truant, disobedient, and showed temper tantrums at the age of 8. Through the interest of a family welfare agency, he was given clinical study, and the mother was given specific instructions for his diet and discipline. His school record improved, but mere instruction and advice could not reinstate parental control.

His school record was one long series of failures. He never went beyond the third grade, although in school from his 5th to his 15th year. Seven terms were spent in grade 1A and 1B. The later school years were spent in an ungraded class, where he did not benefit from his stay, as he was taught nothing that would fit him for industry. He was a truant almost from entrance, and was twice in Truant School.

His mentality, in view of his bad heredity, and his inability to learn, would seem to be defective. Yet when examined in 1917 at the Educational Clinic of the College of the City of New York, his mental age on the Binet scale accorded within a month of his chronological age. He was not regarded as mentally deficient by his teachers.

In 1926, at the age of 17, he was examined at the Lebanon Hospital mental clinic, classified as a high grade moron and characterized as "one of those happy-go-lucky individuals who is subject to suggestion."

Physically, he has always been above above average. He walked at 14 months. At age 8, he was 6 lbs. above normal in weight, and 1½ inches above average in height. He was a vigorous physical specimen until 1923, when at the age of 14, he was operated on for a mastoid infection. Four subsequent operations were necessary, one for empyema. Hearing in his right ear was destroyed. A facial paralysis that still distorts his appearance during speech, resulted. His family has regarded him as a permanent semi-invalid since then, although the activities he indulged in subsequent to his illness point to a complete recovery, and it is probable that the facial paralysis was the infirmity that convinced them of his permanent disability. When last examined, while in the Reformatory his condition was normal except for nasal catarrh.

His interests were always in athletics. While a child he had a bicycle which he frequently rode while absent from school. He occasionally went on excursions with the Settlement House, but the children complained that he fought them. His temper and pugnacity turned in later years into channels that were compensatory for his academic failures. He became a neighborhood bully, and conceived an ambition for pugilism, spending his spare hours in a commercial neighborhood gymnasium that catered to prize fighters.

His personality traits have persisted in set grooves. Throughout school, he was frequently violent in conduct and had chronic bad temper. His illness in 1923 was unfortunate. A bully, and a school failure, be became the pampered "invalid" at home, and was supported in idleness by his parents.

He made the acquaintance of street corner idlers and petty gamblers. Through them he was introduced to pool rooms and later, to cheap dance halls. Influenced by one of them, he made a night raid on a shoe store, and while his more experienced companion opened the show-case and put the shoes in a bag, he stood guard. They were caught entering a taxi with the loot.

Pleading guilty to burglary, 3rd degree, he was placed on probation for 2½ years and put under pressure to do the things he had never done in his life before, namely to work and obey authority. He first worked as an auto mechanic's helper, but quit when the weather grew hot. His employer said the boy was a hard worker, but too unhandy to be of use. He then rode wet-wash laundry wagons with his cronies. In danger of arrest for violation of probation, he secured a job on his father's construction gang, and for several months worked steadily. His pay was $66.00 a week, but of this he received only a few dollars. The remainder was kept by his father, and added to savings for a home he planned to purchase. The big salary at first tickled the boy's vanity and gave him something to brag about to his friends, but when he saw himself getting hardly any of it, he grew angry. Besides, the work prevented him from spending any time with his friends. He therefore disappeared from home, following a quarrel with his father, and rejoined his street gang, taking with him $100 and his newest suit. His apprehension and incarceration followed shortly.

The institution described him as dull, unteachable and unable to acquire information from books. He has fair mechanical capacity, but cannot learn a trade, being lacking in general intelligence. His needs are summarized:

"Is in need of ethical training—should be in the regiment unless disqualified by lack of intelligence. Ought to learn the rudiments of an easy trade but will probably never advance far. Without proper home or institutional supervision, inmate will most likely gravitate into an institution as soon as he is released."

He has been classed among the incorrigibles in the institution, and will be discharged only after 18 months of good behavior.

Discussion: In the case of Peter, the problem of permanent segregation seems to require answer in the negative.

Although characterized as "unteachable" on the basis of his behavior while in the reformatory, his work experience while under court probation showed he could do useful rough labor under supervision.

The crucial point in this case would seem to be the vacillating discipline used by the father. Had some one, by dint of repetition, made the father realize his son's limitations, severity would not have been alternated with coddling. As matters now stand, the son is probably unfavorably conditioned to working under his father's supervision, but intelligent parole ought to consist of another attempt at it, and of an endeavor to have the son obtain a fair proportion of his earnings for his own needs.

What success a parole officer can have with him, on the basis of his institutional experiences, is problematical. The institution officials have not won his confidence or interest. He is incorrigible and will not learn. He is playing the spoiled child behind bars. Does he need "ethical training" or an intelligently directed work program based on the opportunities that will be open to him on his release? Once released, does he not need careful direction of recreation to give him plenty of opportunity for athletic sports among decent company?

Case No. 38—Thomas G., age 19, born April, 1909, in New York City, is now confined in the State Institution for Defective Delinquents, having been convicted in January 1926, of robbery, 1st degree, and grand larceny, 2nd degree.

He comes of Italian parentage. His father, a barber, came to the United States in 1900, nine years before Ferdinand's birth. His mother came here 4 years before his birth. He is third, being preceded by two sisters, and followed by a brother and two sisters.

The parents were married in New York City in 1905. Nothing of their history is known prior to 1921. In this year, they were referred to a family welfare agency by a public school principal, as their rent was past due and they were in danger of eviction. The father was a very sick man, but refused medical aid, and the agency closed the case with the entry "Lack of co-operation."

In 1923, the father died of chronic endocarditis, and the widow appealed to the same agency for aid. She was a difficult person with whom to work, and particularly so at this time, being in a marked depressive state, and weak from a miscarriage.

The mother was an illiterate woman, not even able to sign her name. Prior to her husband's death she assisted by scrubbing floors, and by taking home men's garments, on which she did finishing. She and her husband were characterized by the welfare agency worker as shiftless and very poor in parental control.

The siblings were in poor health. Margaret, the oldest girl, born in 1907, has defective vision, for which she refused care, enlarged tonsils, decayed teeth and a heart murmur. In 1924, she ran away from home, and was not heard of for weeks. She now lives at home and works irregularly. She impressed the Sub-Commission field visitor as dull-looking.

Alegra, born in 1912, was under-nourished, round-shouldered and had enlarged tonsils. She left school while in grade 8-A. She is mentally retarded and gets along poorly at home. A girls' vocational guidance Bureau has made several unsuccessful attempts to place her in employment. She worked only a month or two at jobs she secured herself, in factories. She is now in a factory.

Salvatore, born 1915, is still in school, and apparently no problem.

Lena, born 1916, had decayed teeth and huge tonsils, for which she refused treatment. She was troublesome and a truant. At the age of 12, she is considered attractive and a good dancer. She recently danced in a cheap cabaret and earned $3.00.

Thomas was normal in development except for speech, which began at 25 months. He had scarlet fever, measles and a hernia which should have been operated upon. His school record was neither markedly good nor bad. He was promoted regularly, but was very irregular in attendance, and described as being very disobedient, dishonest and using profane language. He reached grade 8-A at age 16 in the Catholic Protectory.

He belonged to no clubs. He was a member of a street gang, of boys of his type. He was confirmed in the Catholic faith, was regular in attendance, and liked religious services.

He is rated by the Protectory, as dull in intelligence, having an I. Q. of 85. Tested, at the Reformatory, he attained a mental age of only 9 years 2 months. This, on the 16-year adult level in general use, would give him an I. Q. of 60. Using the 14-year level, his I. Q. would be 70. Either rating would classify him as feeble-minded in general abstract intelligence.

Thomas' first court acquaintance was in 1919, at the age of ten, when he was caught, in company with a crowd of other boys, stealing bottles of catsup from a truck. The case was discharged, as the owner did not appear.

In 1920, he was committed to the Truant School, remaining 6 months. Two months later he was re-committed for a period of 5 months. A month later, December 1921, he was caught breaking into a store window and stealing $50.00 in jewelry. He was arraigned in the Children's Court and placed on probation.

In September 1922, he stole a pair of shoes and was committed to the Catholic Protectory. He remained here, except for two brief intervals of unsuccessful parole, 3 years, until September 1925. During this interval his father died. In December 1925, he was held on a robbery charge, and committed to the State Institution for Defective Delinquents.

The home to which he will return was visited by a field visitor of this Sub-Commission. The widowed mother and five children occupy four rooms in a congested neighborhood. The mother is an invalid, suffering from headaches due to her high blood pressure. Her ailment causes her to be unreasonably irritable, and the home atmosphere is quarrelsome. The girls of working age are irregularly employed and the pinch of poverty is constantly felt. The mother considers Thomas quite an intelligent boy! But she describes his attitude toward work as lazy, and his attitude toward supporting the family as indifferent and irresponsible. He is eligible for parole at this writing and will be home almost any day.

Summary: The case speaks for itself. A boy of naturally poor mental endowment, left to shift for himself at a tender age, because of the illness and mental incapacity of his parents, has with the exception of two periods of a year and of 9 months each, spent his boyhood days in correctional institutions. He is now 19. By actual count, in the past nine years, he has spent 5 years and 10 months behind bars. Today or tomorrow he is being dumped on the community, returning to a home broken by death, illness and ignorance, toward whose up-keep he is by past habits not inclined, and handicapped by incapacity and lack of vocational training, in securing employment that will maintain himself alone.

Case No. 39—Samuel G. was born in Austria in 1908. He is now 20, living at home with his parents. He has just been paroled for good behavior from the reformatory where he has been serving a sentence for burglary.

His parents came from Poland 15 years ago, bringing Samuel and an older boy with them.

In 1916, the family came to the charities for relief. The father had been in the hospital, where he was operated upon for an abscess. He was also diabetic, and used his illness as an excuse for shirking work and the responsibility of supporting his family. Though the doctors pronounced him able to do part time work where he could earn $25 and $30 a week, since he was a very good tailor, all attempts to place him were futile. He would complain of aches and pains on the day he was to begin work, and would act so disagreeably on the job that he would be discharged. He was lazy and very willing to let the charities support him.

Several attempts to place him in business were made, for he claimed he was anxious to become self-supporting, but he never made any attempt to find a store or a stand, and used his illness as an excuse for not finding a place. He finally got a pushcart and peddled on the street, selling vegetables.

The mother was a cardiac case and was not able to do much, for she suffered also with varicose veins and flat feet. The filthy condition of the rooms was attributed to her inability to do much work. The five children, when seen, were always dirty and neglected.

They lived in 4 rooms, paying a rental of $22. It was not a pleasant place for the youngsters to grow up in, since the parents were always quarreling, and used reprehensible language to each other in the presence of the children. There was no ethical background, for the parents did not hesitate to lie, and deceit played no small part. They had no control over the children, for they were very impertinent and disrespectful.

In 1923, the oldest boy, a dullard, was working and contributing to the family income, and that added to what the father was earning as vegetable peddler caused the charities to stop aiding them.

In 1928, the family was found living in 4 rooms in a poor neighborhood, rental $35. There are two boys working, and the 3 younger children attend school. One child is a mental defective.

Between February, 1924 and December, 1925, the older son, who is a chauffeur, has been arrested and fined 7 times for violating traffic signals, and for not having a mirror.

Except for Samuel's record, the family is not known to the police.

Samuel's physical condition was not of the best due to his home surroundings. In 1916, he was examined and found to have poor teeth, enlarged tonsils and was undernourished. He and his older brother were referred to a Jewish society and sent to camp during the summer.

His school work was less than average, B and C. His truancy was regular, starting from the very first grade. He was committed to the Truant School for 2 months in 1921 at the age of 13. His truancy was by no means cured, and as a result of hanging around on the streets and in the subway, he was recommitted for another month.

In 1924, at 15, he was arrested for forcing his way into a grocery and stealing $30 in cash, and was committed to a reformatory. While there he tried to escape several times, claiming he wanted to go home and help his family.

When he was examined at Bellevue Hospital in 1924, he was rated as "not a mental defective—no mental trouble." A psychological examination made in 1925 gave him an I. Q. of 112.

He was finally transferred to the House of Refuge in 1925.

In 1927, he was paroled. He has reported regularly and has a good working record.

Discussion: In this case, the example set by the parents was hopeless. Filth, poverty, marital maladjustments, affected the children equally. Yet even here, individual factors enter to make the outcome uncertain. The dull boy has become a responsible working man, and the brighter one has become a jail-bird. Cases such as this illustrate the uselessness of sizing up delinquency problems in merely environmental terms.

In order to know why one boy succeeeded and the other failed, despite similar environmental influences, nothing less than a study of the individual is required.

Case No. 40—Frank O. is the second of twelve children. He was born in 1909, in New York City, and is now 18. He lives away from home, his whereabouts are unknown. He associates with pool room fans, and comes home only when in tatters and penniless. On two occasions recently he has stolen everything at home he could lay hands on, and disappeared. He has had no Children's Court or police record.

The parents, of Italian birth, came to the United States four years before Frank's birth. The family history prior to 1914 is not known. In that year, the parents appealed to a welfare agency for aid.

The father was a barber. He was usually employed, but when out of a job refused to work at any other occupation. Little is known of him save that he was indifferent to his children's truancy, and once was fined in the Municipal Court because of their school absence. His wife claims he has been too lenient with Frank.

Little is known of the mother. She is young in appearance in spite of having borne 12 children and reared 8. Her home has usually been neat and clean. She has been fond of furnishings as elaborate as she could afford. She, too, has been indifferent over the school truancy of her children, her attitude, as expressed to the visitor from a welfare agency, being that she had the right to keep them at home if it suited her convenience. Nor has she been properly concerned over their health. Four have died. One child at present requires a tonsilectomy and has been told by the school authorities not to return until this is done. The mother, in the midst of preparations for a party, stated to the Sub-Commission field visitor, that there was no money to pay a doctor bill. She has been quick to wash her hands of personal responsibilities for the misdemeanors of Frank. When he was truant she insisted he be committed to the Truant School, and now that he is a loafer she does not want to hear from him, and has sought his arrest.

There is no record on the children, other than on Frank, save that Rose, the oldest child, was often kept out of school by the mother to help take care of the smaller children. 3 infants died in 1914, one of diphtheria.

Frank's developmental history is not known. He was already a troublesome boy at the age of 10, according to the mother.

His truancy began in grade 2-B, and continued regularly through grade 5-A, on the average, 30 days a term. His conduct was good and he had little difficulty with his lessons, being retarded only one term up to that time. He was reported as having no bad school habits, but as remaining away from home over night. In 1920 he was committed to the Truant School at his mother's request. Here he remained until March 1921. In June he was recommitted, and this time remained until February 1922. His subsequent record must be reconstructed from the recent interview with the mother.

In December, 1927, the Sub-Commission field visitor found the family living on the 4th floor of a rather clean tenement. The house seemed well furnished. The combination kitchen and dining room was elaborately decorated with many colored crepe papers. They were getting ready for a party. The visitor's report is given verbatim:

"The mother, in spite of having had 12 children (8 living), looked very young. Upon mentioning Frank's name she became very voluble in her curses of him and his doings. 'He was no good—a big bum—a thief—a crook'—has been away now from home over two months. No! I dunno where he is—the last time he came home it was 2 o'clock in the morning and I have shame for the neighbors so I let him in. A regular bum he looked—old clothes—all dirty—and during the night he (Frank) broke open all drawers—stole everything—all money—all jewelry—and denied that he did it—first he bring home a check and say here's money for you but my husband say it's no good—only a piece of paper but Frank say awright, I go bring you money for it but he never come back. After he come out from Protectory he get a job—I dunno where he woik, he give my Domnick a address but he no can find the place and Frank say he never give any news about him to nobody.'

"Frank worked for about 5 or 6 months, contributed $10 to the house but he used up more than that. His mother had to give him 50c every morning, clothe him and feed him. Then suddenly without any excuse or warning he began to absent himself from the home—he would hang out in the pool parlors and with bad companions. Once he came home and stole $20 from the father and when arrested the policeman pleaded for another chance for him but apparently it did no good for only a little while later he returned home and cleaned out everything of any value. The mother has no idea of his whereabouts—has no idea of what kind of work he did—she wanted him put away until he was 21 but the father seemed very lenient and would not agree. She also stated that Frank stole $50 from a friend of the family and the father promised to pay the money back. The father was too good, he never spanked Frank and her only fear is that Frank will get into trouble, real trouble, and there will be no way of getting out of it then.

'And when he come home I get so mad I stick in his heart a knife—better he should be dead so he make no more troubles for me and my family,' the mother declared.

"Yet in spite of all her troubles the place seemed quite festive and she said they were going to have a party.

"Somehow Frank was never out of the mother's mind—he was bad! It was no use trying to help him. He had no love or respect for anybody or anything. When he was 10 years old he said that his mother and his father were nothing to him and he would not abide by anything they might say or do, so she was quite determined to have him put away but again the father was too easy, that's the whole trouble and it's only a 'shame for the neighbors what trouble that boy Frank make.' She did not seem to care as to where the boy would go so long as he did not come home but now she's through and will turn him over to the police if he's found.''

Discussion: This case is illustrative of the parent who doesn't care, and who throws off responsibility at the first opportunity. It is this type of parent who most often winds up a long period of neglect by haling the neglected child into court on a charge of incorrigibility.

There is compulsory education for children, and compulsory commitment for problem cases. Why not compulsory education for parents of problem children?

Case No. 41—Michael C. was born in New York City in 1907. He is now 21 and when last known in 1927 was living with his parents. He has been recently arrested for narcotic sales and is considered a criminal by the police.

The father and mother came from Italy. They are regarded as hard-working honest people and bear a good reputation. The father, a tailor, has worked irregularly and has frequently had to borrow from friends to meet expenses.

The mother raised six children that came at regular intervals of eighteen months and she was occupied with the routine of keeping them washed and fed. In 1914 the children were reported to a welfare agency as being mal-nourished. All had "bow-legs" due to rickets. Until 1916, the family received case work supervision and the father was aided in obtaining employment.

The home consisted of five rooms, and were usually cluttered with rubbish. There were but three beds for eight persons.

None of the family attends church and the children have had no religious training.

The older brothers are very well known to the police. They hang out with a bad Harlem crowd who spend their time in pool rooms and dance halls. The oldest brother, who is now 23, has been apprehended several times for reckless driving, disorderly conduct, burglarly, felonious assault and stabbing. At present he is wanted by the police for participating in ''a hold-up with a gun'' that occurred in a laundry last November.

A younger sister who attended high school, was arrested in 1923 for picking pockets. The mother claimed the girl had no conception of right and wrong, in spite of the fact that the head worker of a settlement house which she attended spoke favorably of her.

Michael spent most of his life upon the street. At the age of 12 he was arrested for loitering in a strange neighborhood during school hours. Up to his fourth year he was promoted steadily, until continued truancy set in. His conduct and proficiency were graded C. A commitment to the Truant School for six months followed. Truancy continued upon his release. He had to repeat each term's work twice and three times and he had only reached the sixth grade when in 1923 he was discharged from school as being over-age.

In 1925, while working as a laborer, he was arrested for disorderly conduct. Hanging around pool rooms, cafes and dance halls brought him into contact with an undesirable element. In 1927 he was charged with a violation of the narcotic act, but acquitted. The police suspect him of being a bootlegger and dope-peddler.

Case No. 42—Stephen T., now 21, was born in New York City in 1907. He is now serving an indeterminate term in the penitentiary for assault and robbery.

The parents were born in Italy. Their children, four girls and two boys, were all born in the United States. The family has always been self-supporting and has not been known to philanthropic agencies. The home, which has been maintained in a congested foreign quarter, consists of four rooms which have been kept moderately clean.

All of the children, save the youngest who is attending school, are of working age, are employed, and have no police records. The oldest boy earns $20 a week as a truck driver for a paper box firm. One girl works in a paper box factory, another as a stenographer. Stephen, up to the time of his arrest, worked as a baker's helper, earning $25 a week.

Stephen appears to have been the black sheep of the family. Early in life he got into trouble and since has been under police surveillance. In school, his record was very poor. Truancy began in the first grade and continued throughout school life. He stole, was ill-behaved in the class-room, and was fond of "picking fights" with the other pupils. He showed no interest in his studies, constantly received C in proficiency, and repeated every term at least twice. At the age of 10, he was committed to the Truant School, and transferred to the Catholic Protectory. At 11, he was sent to the Catholic Protectory for petty thieving. At 13, he was sent for a period of eight months to the Parental School, for truancy. After this, he went from bad to worse, and associated with bad companions, who drank to excess. At the age of 16, he was sent to the House of Refuge for stealing an auto. Upon his release, he sought out his friends and was shortly afterward apprehended for assaulting and attempting to rob a stranger. He was sentenced to the penitentiary.

His work services were satisfactory, according to the few employers interviewed by court probation officers. His parents claimed he contributed his entire salary while he was working. On the other hand, they supported him during his periods of idleness.

The police report that his criminal experience has made him very wise in police methods, and on his last arrest he tried every trick and artifice, ably aided by his family, to evade trial. He was hardened in attitude and evasive. He is regarded as a confirmed thief. His forte consists of robbing drunken men—lush work—and he was engaged in this when last apprehended. His method consists of striking and choking his victims, and then relieving them of their valuables.

Discussion: When Stephen T. was a child, his school playmates complained of his fondness for striking them. At 21, he is a confirmed criminal, whose method consists of striking and choking his victims. Thus has a neglected childhood trait developed into a menace. Habit-training during his school career might have inhibited this cruel tendency. His commitments to various institutions failed to do it.

Case No. 43—John S., age 21, is serving a term in the Penitentiary, having been convicted of stealing a tire from an automobile. He has the reputation of being a petty thief.

The family history is not known, save in the sketchiest of outlines.

The parents, who were born in Italy, have both been dead for ten years or more, and the family of 9 children has been scattered. When the father lived, he owned a grocery store on the East Side.

The oldest son a man of 32, lives in a prosperous Brooklyn neighborhood, in a well-furnished home. With him are two sisters, ages 14 and 15, who from 1920 to 1925 were in an orphanage. They are described as retarded in school and only of fair mentality. He has been interviewed, but was reluctant to give information, apparently ashamed of his family connections. That which he did give has been checked from another source and found to be accurate.

One boy, unidentified, has been in an orphanage.

A sister is married and lives on the East Side in a pleasant 4 room apartment.

John's developmental history and boyhood life are not known, except that from the reports of the Bureau of Attendance, one gathers that he lived with an older member of the family, in a poor tenement neighborhood, in a well-furnished home, however. There was indifferent supervision over him.

His school career extended through grade 6B. He was retarded 6 terms. His work ranged from B to C, and his conduct was A in the early grades, but B and C when he was most frequently a truant. His school absences were frequent, beginning with grade 1A. In grade 4B, he was away on an average of 50 full days per term. He spent 2 years in grade 4B, in part while in the Truant School, where he was committed, from December 1918 to June 1919, and from September 1919 to March 1920.

His school record improved somewhat following his parole, but in June 1921 he was again committed, remaining until December. A last short commitment followed in February, 1922. In October, he was discharged from school as being 16 and no longer required to attend.

The school description of his behavior is negligible. His conduct is rated as poor, he smoked, and played on the street.

His work record is unknown, except that he secured a driver's license, as in May 1925, he paid a fine in Traffic Court for making an improper turn.

In December, 1927, a field visitor learned from his oldest brother, that John is now married to an Italian girl and has lived somewhere on the Lower East Side. He stated that John always was a problem, ran away from home several times, and has not profited by friendly advice, showing remorse only for a day or so, and then returning to his old haunts and friends on the East Side. He has no regular occupation, never wanted an education and thought more of his gangs than his family. The brother feels he is beyond redemption.

In January, 1928, the Detective Bureau of the New York Police Department gave the following statement on its inquiry into the boy's record:

"John is well known to the detectives of the X precinct. He is in their estimation of low mentality, a general thief, and is thoroughly bad. He is now in the Penitentiary, having been sent there in October, 1927, for stealing a tire from an auto. He has been arrested several times before. He is held responsible for a number of store burglaries, and petty thefts in the neighborhood, but the detectives did not have sufficient evidence to arrest him. These thefts ceased after he was sent away. Last summer he ran away with a 16 year old girl and married her. She is now with her mother."

Discussion: The casual manner in which a number of the boys in this group were married is worthy of attention. Child-marriages under any circumstance have grave handicaps, but for the state to countenance legal unions of the sort described is folly. In John's case, the endless circle of delinquent child and delinquent parent is unfolding itself before our eyes. It would be interesting to know whether the Penitentiary to which he has been committed is aware that he is a husband and will probably become a father, and if it is aware of this, what interest its officials have in preparing him for his responsibilities.

Case No. 44—William B. was born in New York City in 1905. He is 23 now and lives with is father and two younger brothers. He drives a truck but has no regular job, working for his friends "now and then," mostly "then."

His parents came from Italy in 1885. The five children, 3 boys and 2 girls were all born in this country. The father worked as a laborer and does not appear to have earned much. Although he has been in this country 43 years, he speaks very, very little English. When seen by a visitor from this Sub-Commission, he could not answer any question but conveyed his meaning by using his hands and pointing at various objects. He was very dirtily clad and looked as if soap and water were alien to his make-up. He appeared to be literally sewed up in his clothes. It was learned that he has not been out of the house in 3 years, since the death of his wife. He is waiting to die in the same rooms.

Little is known of him and the mother, except that there must have been standards of loyalty for the children do what they can to support him. He has not been working for several years. Judging by the condition of the rooms it is unlikely that any sort of decent hygiene was ever taught or used. It is not known how long William's people have lived in the neighborhood.

When visited in 1927 the home consisted of three dirty smelly rooms on the 4th floor of a tenement. No running water, except a pump handle sink in the hall, used by 4 families. There were two bed rooms, no ventilation, plaster broken in several places. No linens on the beds. Dirty rags hanging everywhere. A very strong odor of mash pervaded the hall and the rooms. Bottles of beer in the hall and on the fire escape. Clothes boiling on an old wood stove; coffee cooking on a one light gas stove. The place was not only poorly furnished but very, very dirty.

The two younger boys do the housekeeping when they come home from work. No information concerning any of their activities could be gotten. They too are irregularly employed.

When the mother died in 1925 the two girls left the home. The oldest who was married, felt it unwise to leave the younger girl alone with the men of the family, so she has made her home with the married sister. They come to visit the old man and have tried everything to get him to leave the place but he cannot be prevailed upon to change his mind. He simply refuses to budge.

At 14, William was arrested for stealing from stores but was put on probation. In 1920 at 15 he was again apprehended for burglary and again put in probation. At 16, in 1921, he was committed to the Truant School for three months and then placed on probation. No definite record of any of his school work is known. We can only surmise his dislike for learning and the time he spent with the gang on the street. Between his 17th and 19th year he worked as a laborer of some kind and was arrested for playing crap. In 1923 he worked as a chauffeur—there is no way of telling how he learned the trade nor where—but he got in with a bootlegger and was arrested for having whiskey in his possession. During 1924–1925 he was arrested and fined four times for violating traffic rules. He was not interested in obeying rules and according to his last arrest in 1927, he was caught violating the Volstead Act but nothing was done about it.

At noon, the visitor found William still in bed. He made no effort to get up or get dressed. He was good-natured and willing to talk.

William is strongly built, heavy features make him look stupid. He appears lazy and slovenly, is a little hard of hearing and has a distinct adenoid condition. He said that he went to the clinic but had no patience to stand in line and so came home. He spends his spare time hanging around the streets with the boys, or in the cafes which are very numerous in his neighborhood. He does not go to church but goes to a show when he has the money. He states that he would work regularly but resents being bossed for only $35 or $40 a week. "Those fellers what work in offices with a pencil get $15 a day." His ignorance equals his sense of values. He looks for a job when he gets up, usually after noon. Most of his friends he claims are in the trucking business, bootleggers probably. He also claimed that he was working on a radio invention of his own and had put most of his earnings into it but finally lost patience. "Got disgusted and bust the thing."

He has an insurance policy that he would be glad to sell, and cannot understand why he is unable to save any money.

Discussion: William has been "on his own" for a number of years, and has kept out of jail, thanks to Prohibition and its lucrative byproduct, boot-legging. Many persons have claimed that the only way to put the adult criminal out of the way of temptation is to provide him with work that will equal what he can gain out of crime. In this case at least, society has demonstrated the soundness of that claim. But should boot-legging cease to be profitable, then William must have a bank presidency. Seriously, however, William and his mode of living raise a most perplexing question. A certain number of youngsters are always torn between small honest wages and large dishonest profits. In any event, unless he is a skilled mechanic, economic uncertainty is about the same. What shibboleths can those utter who must persuade him in the direction of honesty? What can they do to overcome a cynicism born of experience and the tabloids?

TABLES

SECTION I. OFFENSES COMMITTED

Table		PAGE
I.	Present age of all offenders, by groups	20
II.	Birthplace of parents	21
III.	Total of arraignments, by groups	22
IV.	Proportion of arraignments by type of offense	23
V.	Nature of juvenile delinquencies, by groups	33
VI.	Misdemeanors by number and type of offense	33
VII.	Felonies by type of offense	34
VIII.	Arraignments and convictions, by groups	35
IX.	Disposition of cases, by groups	35

SECTION II. SOCIAL FACTORS

X.	Nativity of offenders and parents	37
XI.	Nativity of offenders and parents, by degree of delinquency	40
XII.	Nativity of males and females in Manhattan, 1920	41
XIII.	Recency of immigration among parents of offenders	42
XIV.	Number of children in family in relation to type of offense	43
XV.	Family position of offender	43
XVI.	Income in relation to type of offense	44
XVII.	Income per person in relation to type of offense	45
XVIII.	Occupation of mother	46
XIX.	Civil Status of home	46
XX.	Size of dwelling	48
XXI.	Degree of housing congestion	48
XXII.	Number of social service agencies registered on families	49
XXIII.	Type of agencies registered on families	50
XXIV.	Philanthropic services rendered	50
XXV.	Mobility	51
XXVI.	Police record for others in family	52
XXVII.	Extent of criminal record among families of offenders	52
XXVIII.	Arraignments among members of families of truants	53
XXIX.	Arraignments among members of families of delinquents	53
XXX.	Arraignments among members of families of misdemeanants	54
XXXI.	Arraignments among members of families of felons	54

SECTION III. BEHAVIOR FACTORS

XXXII.	Onset of truancy	55
XXXIII.	Relative amount of truancy	56
XXXIV.	School conduct ratings	57
XXXV.	School proficiency ratings	58
XXXVI.	Grade reached	58
XXXVII.	Gang affiliation	59
XXXVIII.	Degree of skill in position held	59
XXXIX.	Type of job held	61

THE UNIVERSITY OF MICHIGAN

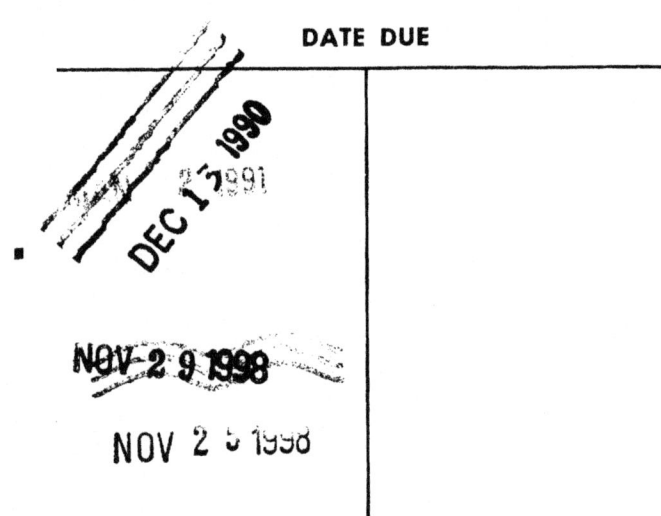

DO NOT REMOVE
OR
MUTILATE CARD

9/70 AFRidout